John,
Appreciate how you are
leading the way to make
our entry
look "easy"
into
Enterprise
IT

Best, Bob

CRAFTING PERSUASION

The Leader's Handbook to
Change Minds and Influence Behavior

Kip Knight, Ed Tazzia & Bob Pearson

Other books by Ed Tazzia

Starting Over

One Guy, Two Perspectives on
Losing a Job and Finding a New One

Other books by Bob Pearson

PreCommerce

Storytizing

Countering Hate

(with Haroon K. Ullah)

Crafting Persuasion
Kip Knight, Ed Tazzia & Bob Pearson
ISBN: 978-0-9996623-4-2
Copyright © 2019 by 1845 Publishing

Cover photo © eight8 for Adobe Stock.com
Cover and interior design by Monica Thomas for TLC Book Design,
TLCBookDesign.com

Printed in the United States of America.

TABLE OF CONTENTS

Introduction: Could You Please Come to the White House?................**7**

Chapter 1   The Foundation of Communication Strategy—
            What's Your Model?................**11**

    Sidebar: Strategy Before Execution, by Norm Levy 18

Chapter 2   Simple as A, B, C................**21**

    Sidebar: Don't Underestimate the Power of the ABCDE Model,
    by Dave Wallinga 35

Chapter 3   'A' Is for Audience................**37**

    Sidebar: The Three Most Important Things to Remember About
    Consumer Research, by Dr. Jim Nyce................60

Chapter 4   'B' Is for Behavioral Objective **65**

    Sidebar: Best Advice? Put Emotions and Feelings First,
    by Dr. Victoria Romero................75

Chapter 5   'C' Is for Content **77**

    Sidebar: Focus on the Key Message, by Kimberly Doebereiner................90

Chapter 6   'D' Is for Delivery................**91**

    Sidebar: How to Get Great Work from Your Creatives, by Elena Gold.....108

Chapter 7   'E' Is for Evaluation **111**

    Sidebar: The Three Fundamentals for Measuring Communications
    Performance, by Chuck Hemann................121

Chapter 8   The Power of Persuasion................**123**

    Sidebar: How to Persuade a Tough Audience, by Mike Linton............134

Chapter 9   Connecting with Youth................**137**

    Sidebar: Five Core Truths About Innovation, by Doug Hall................158

Chapter 10 Digital Marketing... **161**

Sidebar: Social Media—The Opportunities and Challenges Ahead,
   by Gary Briggs... 169

Chapter 11 Issues Management.. **171**

Sidebar: How Diplomats Persuade Hostile Audiences,
   by Teeta Manson 183

Chapter 12 Case Studies—
             From Startups to Fortune 500 Companies **185**

Sidebar: Three Keys to Effective Marketing Across Culture, Country,
   and Time, by Rob Malcolm 204

Chapter 13 Non-Business Case Studies................................. **205**

Sidebar: How to Create Loyalty Among Non-Loyal Audiences,
   by Kelly Hlavinka 220

Chapter 14 Heads Up—Common Pitfalls to Avoid................. **223**

Sidebar: How to Guard Against Someone Hijacking Your Message,
   by Klon Kitchen.. 234

Chapter 15 The Road Ahead **237**

Acknowledgments **243**

About the authors.. **244**

Introduction:
Could You Please Come to the White House?

> **"Necessity is the mother of invention."**
> −Plato

Some phone calls you never forget. The call Kip Knight received on an otherwise normal weekday night in May 2008 was one of them.

Kip was relaxing in his study, catching up on work from his job as one of eBay's vice presidents, when the phone rang. The person on the line identified herself as Jody Moxham, the president of an agency that worked with the National Security Council. She asked if he'd be willing to travel to Washington D.C. and meet with some NSC officials, who wanted to figure out ways to burnish the country's image abroad.

If you ask Kip today, he can't recall if he actually pulled the phone away from his ear and looked at it incredulously, but he certainly felt that way. He and Jody talked for a few minutes before he asked her for a little time to think about it. As unusual and improbable as the request was, it was a legitimate and important one.

Kip thought such a meeting would be, at worst, an interesting learning experience. So, he told them he would fly in from California to participate.

After all, it's not every day that a marketer who didn't serve in the military gets a call from the government: "Your country could really use your help right now." To this day, Kip has no idea why they asked him—despite asking several times—but the request opened an incredible new pathway.

Kip had spent his career selling soap, tacos and a variety of other products, leading traditional and e-commerce marketing efforts for some of the world's most respected companies, including P&G, PepsiCo and eBay. Marketing the United States as a brand was something he'd never even imagined.

The NSC, however, had become increasingly alarmed by the beating the U.S. brand was taking around the world. The Iraq War was dragging into its fifth year, and expectations for a quick victory had vanished. Still reeling from the Abu Ghraib prison scandal four years earlier, and mired in a conflict that had no end in sight, the NSC officials wondered whether some professional marketers could help improve the country's reputation abroad.

So, about a month after Jody first called, Kip and marketing experts from two other Fortune 500 companies found themselves sitting in the White House Cabinet Room across from the Oval Office. For the next hour, Kip and his colleagues fielded basic questions about how various U.S. agencies should think about marketing strategy, as well as the latest developments in digital marketing and social media (which, back in 2008, was still in its infancy).

The marketers in the room noted the irony that the United States, home to many of the best marketing teams in the world, couldn't take all that collective experience and talent and apply it to improve the country's image abroad. There was consensus that the State Department, the agency primarily responsible for maintaining and enhancing the U.S. brand, lagged what most U.S. corporations were doing. At many embassies, holding a press conference and distributing a press release remained the primary means of communication.

As the meeting closed, Kip was dubious. The gathering had been interesting, he told the group, but he didn't think it would make any difference in improving the country's current image. What *would* move the needle significantly, he said, would be if teams such as those in the State

Department were given strategic training, so they could craft and carry out truly effective communication strategies.

Kip had put on training seminars for marketing teams at PepsiCo and eBay. What if you could bring together some of the best marketers in the country to teach government officials how to think more strategically about messaging? Already there in the room, he'd been processing a few variables that would make this assignment especially demanding:

- The U.S. State Department interacts with 195 countries with widely varying governments and cultures.
- The global population speaks more than 8,300 languages.
- At the time, the world population was 6.7 billion people.

A "marketplace" this vast meant the teaching team would have to take years of marketing wisdom and boil it down into a simple, scalable model that could work as easily in Uzbekistan or Niger as it could in Brazil or, for that matter, Boston. Kip knew he and his long-time colleagues were up to the task. He offered to mount this effort on a pro bono basis. To his surprise, he got a green light.

Out of necessity, a new communication strategy model reflecting decades of work was about to be born.

CHAPTER 1

The Foundation of Communication Strategy— What's Your Model?

> **"The advancement and diffusion of knowledge is the only guardian of true liberty."**
> –James Madison

James Madison, the fourth president of the United States (1809–1817), is widely regarded as the father of the U.S. Constitution for the important role he played in creating and, quite frankly, marketing both this founding charter and the Bill of Rights to his fellow citizens.

Both documents remain true to this very day. They constitute the core foundation of our country and continue to guide how we, as Americans, think and act worldwide. Our founders realized that "scaling" their new model of Democracy would be critical to the country's long-term success. Based on the two and a half centuries that followed the launch of their "campaign," you could make a pretty convincing argument that Madison and his fellow framers were more than just great political thinkers—they were darn good marketers, too.

For our new assignment with the State Department and other government agencies, we sought to create an effective communication model that could, like the country's founding documents, scale and stand the test of time. Over the years, we developed a curriculum that eventually led to the model we lay out in this book. We believe this model can scale to help enable our current leaders to promote ideas, policies and positions needed for all of us to succeed in a modern world. In fact, we've already seen it work across a wide variety of situations, including businesses and non-profits. The core strategic communication principles work, regardless of the type of organization.

Now, we weren't crazy enough to think we were creating anything so august as the U.S. Constitution, but we did realize that what we developed would be shared by many others. So, it had to be memorable, foundational and easy to implement anywhere in the world. It had to work across cultures in 195 different countries and via thousands of different languages. Simple stuff.

So, the work began, starting with what to call these courses we would be teaching to State Department staff and their colleagues. As a marketer of a new brand, one of the first things you need is a name. Kip called several of his marketing colleagues, including Ed Tazzia, with whom he worked at P&G. Since we weren't naming a new consumer packaged goods brand, we decided to keep the name simple and clear. It also needed to capture the goal: to train key U.S. government officials in the art and science of marketing, so they could better craft their message to key target audiences. We decided to call the classes the United States Marketing Communication College (USMCC), knowing it would end up with the nickname "Marketing College."

The USMCC would bring together a group of marketing professionals, each with years of experience leading U.S. companies, and put them in front of a weeklong class of about 40 "students"—State Department and other agency officials who worked at posts spanning the globe. The faculty would include a range of professional expertise, including Dr. Victoria Romero, a neuroscience expert, Dr. Jim Nyce, former head of market research for Kraft and Sun Products, and Bob Pearson, a pioneer in new digital models and algorithms as part of his work at W2O, a leading digital marketing agency.

We wanted our time with our students to be as interactive and engaging as possible. Over time, we would cover topics such as marketing strategy, crisis communication, youth marketing and social media. In addition, we would invite our "students" to send us some real-world problems they were dealing with that we could discuss in class. (This exercise eventually led to a more formal process in which students would write up a case study on a communication problem they were grappling with back at their embassy or consulate in order to be invited to the college.) We would ask groups of students to work on developing an effective communication plan to address their issues, knowing some of these case studies could be successfully executed once the students returned to their current assignments. We figured this would be outstanding evidence that the training really worked.

Right from the start, we focused on the scalability and practicality of what we were trying to do. Would what we were teaching find its way to the local audiences of our students and thus improve how we share, shape and tell our country's story around the world?

We were ready to find out as the first classes approached, but we knew we would need to heed Gen. Eisenhower's observation: "Plans are useless, but planning is indispensable." The only way we could know if this training program was going to work was to hold the initial session with government personnel from all over the world and see what they thought of it. Three months after the initial meeting in the White House, the inaugural class of the Marketing College gathered in Arlington, Virginia, on the campus of the Foreign Service Institute (the training center for the State Department).

Business professionals are from Mars... government professionals are from Venus

Despite our extensive preparation, the first USMCC session in August of 2008 quickly revealed three major challenges we would have to overcome.

First, there was real confusion about the separation between policy creation and communication strategy. Creating policy for the United States is certainly important and critical, but that was not what we were there for. We had to remain policy neutral and keep our focus on teaching everyone how to clearly communicate policy to the intended audience. To put it in business terms, we had to help the team enhance their ability to market the product, not suggest what the product should look like.

Second, this was the first time that many of our students spent any time working with marketing experts from the business world. Many of the examples we wanted to use from our business experience were going to be hard to translate for those who had spent an entire career in the government.

The third challenge was the most intimidating: How would we convince students, many of them with years of experience dealing with extremely challenging assignments in tough places, to put the development of a communications *strategy* before *execution*? Most of the people we were working with were used to immediately executing on a message their boss asked for. Getting them and their bosses to start with development of a communication strategy first was a tall order.

The critical importance of putting strategy ahead of execution

This dilemma was understandable. When you work at a U.S. embassy and the ambassador asks for a press release or wants you to set up a press conference, it's a challenge to push back and ask what the overall communication strategy should be—especially if your superiors don't even know what an effective communication strategy looks like.

The reason putting strategy ahead of execution is so critical is because strategy is *what* you are trying to communicate to an audience. Execution is *how* you are going to communicate it. You have to decide *what* you want to say before you decide *how* you want to say it. And you have to be sure everyone involved agrees on the *what* before you spend time and resources developing and executing the *how*.

It might sound obvious that strategy should come before execution. But if an organization never developed a strategy as part of its overall communication process—or if organization leaders think everyone already understands the strategy—serious problems can arise. Organizations create and reinforce habits that often have to change. A focus on tactics first is a prime example. Ready, shoot, aim won't get you consistent results, but it's easy to forget what otherwise sounds like common sense when you've been ordered to roll out a new campaign in a hurry. You are so busy you don't stop to consider if your efforts are making a long term, significant impact

Here's another way to think about it: If someone gave you $10 million to build your dream house, would you immediately go out and hire a bunch of construction workers? Of course not—you would work with an architect first. You would talk about your hopes and dreams for the future with all the people who were going to live in that house. You would all agree on a grand vision for what it would look like before the first nail was hammered.

Developing an effective communication plan is no different. You need to make sure you've made the important strategic decisions first. Who are you targeting? What do you want them to do? Why should they believe you? And so on. Only after you've gotten your strategy together and secured agreement from the other stakeholders should you begin to develop an execution plan.

Unfortunately, creating and leveraging a communication strategy takes time and is hard work, but it's absolutely worth the effort. The question for those of us on the USMCC faculty was how we could help our students do this in a powerful and pragmatic manner.

Ten years later...

Despite a somewhat shaky start, we've now held USMCC training sessions for more than a decade. We're like the Farmers Insurance commercial that says, "We know a thing or two because we've seen a thing or two." (One of our faculty members, Mike Linton, is the chief marketing officer at Farmers Insurance, and he knows a thing or two about marketing!)

The results have been well beyond what any of us would have imagined when we started this journey in 2008. We've used the feedback and evaluations from every session over the past 10-plus years to make both small tweaks and significant overhauls. We had to learn—and accept—that some of our ideas wouldn't scale so well in certain environments or where the necessary budget might not be available. Yet, over time, we created a process and framework that works.

As of 2018, we have trained more than 700 diplomats, government officials and staff from nongovernmental organizations (NGOs) who work in
embassies, in consulates and with various U.S.-partner organizations in
locations around the world. We hear from many of our former students on
a regular basis, often when they need an outside perspective on a particular communication issue they face.

In our course evaluations, which we make sure to gather after every
session, many participants have said this is some of the best and most
pragmatic training they have received in their entire career—and some of
these professionals have spent more than 30 years in their U.S. government
roles. To receive that kind of testimonial makes this work worthwhile on
its own, but we're more thankful for how our students shape the ways we
reconceive and enhance our curriculum.

Three challenges, three solutions

So how did we handle the three big challenges we faced in that first
USMCC session? As Eisenhower's observation foretold, we had to immediately make some adjustments and retool our initial approach. But we
also had to keep planning, as we've continued to do over the past decade:

- **Policy versus communication strategy**—This was fairly easy. We
  made it crystal clear, to ourselves and our students, that we would
  have nothing to do with developing or debating policy in our classes.
  There were plenty of others in the government who already dedicated
  their professional careers to policy development. We would leave that
  complex challenge to the experts. Our focus would be on showing
  our students how to effectively communicate a policy, regardless of
  who created it, to a target audience.

- **Business versus government**—Over the years, we got better at
  making sure professionals who work in government can understand
  and relate to our communication examples from the business world.
  We also make sure each business example is relevant to the students,
  so they can see a clear connection between it and what they regularly
  face in their professional world. More important, perhaps, we've
  worked hard as a faculty to cross that business-government gap,

significantly increasing the number of case studies we draw directly from NGOs and government.

- **Communication execution versus communication strategy—** This remains our most persistent challenge. The tendency to put execution ahead of strategy is not limited to the State Department or other government agencies; it's a universal problem. Way too often when faced with a communication or marketing challenge, people have a strong bias to take immediate action. Without a strategic foundation for execution, the odds of success decrease dramatically.

It is this ongoing challenge that inspired us, after a decade of teaching about communication strategy, to write this book. Our model provides a robust strategic framework for how to tell your story in a powerful way for any business, government, NGO or nonprofit organization.

We call it the ABCDE Communication Model.

Strategy Before Execution

Norm Levy
Original Director, Advertising Development, The Procter & Gamble Company

Consider this truism: The most brilliant execution of a flawed strategy is likely to fail. (This is true in military battles and in marketing.) A brilliant execution of a right strategy has immense value.

The principle to be extracted here is this: Efforts devoted to informed strategic development are the foundation of effective communication. In a communications context, "strategy" defines *what* a message will contain (ideas, promises, benefits). "Execution" deals with *how* that message content will be delivered (words, pictures, style, dramatic *values*).

My observation, based on a very long career working with clients and advertising agencies, is that enormous amounts of energy and time are wasted by leaping to the executional expressions before the strategy has been adequately formulated and *agreed to* by the participants in the creative and approval process. So what?

- **Time and money are lost:** Needless work is generated by revisions traceable to "changes in direction." This happens when execution work is not based on a set of objectives previously agreed to by the participants in the approval process (various levels of management at both client and ad agency).

- **Creative enthusiasm and focus is diminished:** Creative energy is "turned off" when creative people who have honestly responded to an assumed strategy find that their work is zeroed-out because of a shift in strategic direction (often because some manager who is part of the approval was not exposed to the "strategy" at its formative stage).

In addition to helping you avoid wasting time and energy the "strategy before execution" approach gives you and your teams two key advantages:

- **Discipline:** Creative effort will, from the start, be focused on transforming the most informed strategic thinking into interesting, persuasive, and dramatic executions.

- **A faster creative development and approval:** With a well thought out *written* communications strategy in-hand, all participants literally start out on the same page. In today's business structures, participants are often widely distributed geographically, so the need to be aligned on strategy is vital. In the approval process, a communications strategy document will serve as a reminder of the specific objectives as participants exercise their personal judgements.

The ABCDE approach to the development of a communications strategy is a simple, intuitively logical, and successful construct that will help you put strategy before execution.

Try it! ■

CHAPTER 2

Simple as A, B, C

> "We have the right to our own opinions,
> but not our own facts."
>
> –Former U.S. Senator Daniel Patrick Moynihan

A strong strategic plan centers on facts and evolves from there. Opinions take us in any direction we want, often not good. As we taught the Marketing College classes, we realized that despite continual reminders from faculty members to start with strategy, students who were working on their case studies wanted to jump immediately into an execution plan. They were certain a new Facebook campaign, supplemented with Twitter and Instagram messaging, would work perfectly—without ever having confirmed the audience, the situation or the objective.

In addition to those who tended to hone in on digital and online activities, we always had some students who wanted to hold live events. (Beyoncé was the celebrity of choice, and somehow our students were willing to assume she'd do a free concert in some remote part of the world to support their cause.) There would be press conferences, radio commercials, public relations campaigns and so on.

These discussions frustrated the faculty. We knew our students would never have the kind of money, expertise and marketing resources we had available at large private-sector companies. But even if they had all the money and resources in the world, it would not matter if they didn't start with a solid definition of their goals. The differing backgrounds of our faculty members[1] only compounded our collective frustrations. While we all had worked at companies with similar communication strategy development processes, we initially lacked a common terminology. Until we had one, we would have a difficult time teaching students how to create their own communication strategies.

So, we set out to establish standards and develop a model that would reinforce those standards. If you are a chief financial officer, for example, you practice the Generally Accepted Accounting Principles (GAAP) standards. If you are a chief technology officer, you use widely accepted standard security protocols to help secure your critical database. But if you are a chief marketing, chief communications or chief digital officer, welcome to the Wild Wild West! Standards hardly exist. If our Marketing College training was going to have any lasting impact in our students' worlds, we desperately needed to develop a "strategic communication roadmap" for them to use on a regular basis.

Ed Tazzia had chipped away on this huge problem for several years when it finally occurred to him: We needed something simple enough to remember and use without looking it up. It needed to be easily explained and illustrated. And it needed to be based on what we know can work in the real world. In the end, it was a student who suggested the first five letters of the alphabet as the framework for this model. The ABCDE Communication Model had a name—progress!

When Ed struck on this as a communication strategy framework, we finally had something we could put into practice. A lot of this model is based upon work initiated at P&G, which remains one of the world's largest advertisers with an annual advertising budget of more than $7.1 billion (USD). But, given the professional diversity of our faculty, we also

---

1   The USMCC faculty has included representatives from Procter & Gamble, Google, Facebook, Mattel, Best Buy, Farmers Insurance, PepsiCo, Hilton, IBM, eBay, Kraft and Diageo, among others.

made sure it was consistent with the approaches other organizations took when crafting communication strategy.

Overview of the ABCDE Communication Model

The beauty of the ABCDE model is rooted in its simplicity, which makes it effective in various situations—including different companies, countries, and environments. We'll dive into much more detail in the coming chapters but, let's start simple: Here's what the ABCDE abbreviation stands for:

- **Audience**—Who is your message aimed at?

- **Behavioral objective**—What do you want them to do?

- **Content**—What is in your communication strategy (e.g., benefits, reason to believe, tone and character)?

- **Delivery**—How do you plan to deliver your intended communication strategy (both the message itself and the communication channels you use)?

- **Evaluation**—How will you assess your campaign's impact?

We're enthusiastic about this model because, while it is simple to explain and remember, it provides a powerful process to ensure you think through all the key elements of an effective communication strategy. It's what we like to call a "strategic filter"—great models allow you to reflect on what you are doing, immediately identify important missing pieces, and show you how to get to where you want to go. It helps you filter your thinking, and as you do that you begin to see why the model works so well.

The ABCDE Communication Model

Can marketing make a difference? Just ask Steve Jobs, or the Rev. Dr. Martin Luther King Jr., or the leaders of ISIS. They're vastly different people with sharply divergent, often conflicting messages, yet they share an ability to communicate persuasively and solicit the response they desire. A slight tweak of the ABCDE concepts we listed above can transform them from a plan for marketing a new commercial product or service to an effective strategy for almost any message that involves:

- developing the **right** proposition
- to reach the **right** target
- with the **right** value
- and the **right** positioning, execution plan and communication channels.

When building a marketing program with multiple parts—events, advertising, public relations, web presence, etc.—it's imperative that you take the time to connect these dots and ensure each piece builds toward the same promise. Each interaction with your audience, even things over which you have no control, influences how your audience perceives and values your promise. Making sure every aspect and audience touch-point supports your strategy helps accelerate the return on your investment of time, resources, money and staffing.

This proven approach grows out of billions of dollars of marketing, market research and consumer response that multinational corporations have invested over the past 80-plus years. No matter what communication challenge you have, this model works.

Audience

The first question any marketer or communicator should always ask themselves is this: "Who am I trying to persuade?" You can use a variety of parameters to define your audience—demographics, psychographics, behavioral, etc. However, behavior is perhaps the most important sorting criterion for your target audience.

The ultimate objective of a communication campaign is to elicit a desired behavior—whether that behavior is purchasing your product or turning away from violent extremist organizations. One might think of an audience the way politicians think about voters in their districts. If you're running for public office, you can classify potential voters into one of three groups:

- **Loyalists**—Congratulations! These folks (such as your mom) are going to vote for you *no matter what.*
- **Detractors**—Sorry, but these people are *never* going to vote for you. Trying to get their vote is only going to make them even more irritated with you than they already are, and it's going to burn up scarce and valuable resources.

- **The Middle (or "Movable")**—These are the voters who are going to make you or break you, assuming your loyalists or your detractors haven't become the majority already. You and your campaign manager are going to need to focus on "moving the middle"—getting enough of these undecided voters to support you on Election Day.

Just as an earnest politician tries to win by "moving the middle," you are trying to persuade your audience. It's up to you to understand who in your audience is open to being persuaded, as well as the best ways to identify those people.

Importantly, an indirect approach can work best. For example, you can start by determining who influences your ultimate audience. Who does your audience depend on to provide information, give counsel and guide their thinking? Once you know who helps your target audience members make their important decisions, it might work best to focus your initial messages on these key influencers. It often can be more efficient and effective, especially if one person influences many.

Your target audience members will change and evolve over time. Part of this shift will occur naturally, as they grow, mature and become exposed to new ideas. Part of the change will stem from your own making, as you decide to vector to another strategy or sub-strategy. Ideally, you make these changes deliberately, rather than reacting to the marketplace, the competition or the environment.

Deciding who you are focusing your message on requires a layered discussion with several dimensions. There are **strategic targets**, a group that includes individuals who might find your message relevant and meaningful. There are **prime prospects**, a subset of the strategic targets who represent the greatest near-term opportunities for successful responses to our behavioral objectives. In the commercial world, the strategic target for a hotel chain might include all potential travelers. But prime prospects might include business travelers, vacation travelers, value travelers, or luxury travelers. You can begin to see how that hotel chain might customize its message for each subset of its prime prospects.

Another dimension would be understanding the influencers or the key "gatekeepers" for your ultimate audience. Historically, if you were trying to sway a group of United Auto Workers, you might try to sway their union leadership with the objective of having them try to influence your broader strategic targets on your behalf. If you are trying to convince someone in a family to purchase your product or program, you must know who makes the actual purchase decision versus who uses the product. If you want to convince a young African high school student to come to the United States to study, it may well be that you need to convince the real decision maker—the mother—of the value of your proposal.

While this might seem obvious, we can point you to dozens of failed programs that did not take these audience decisions into consideration. In Chapter 3, we'll discuss these and other consumer insights in more detail, discussing why they are important and how to generate that audience knowledge. Consumer insights aren't gleaned simply by gathering data. There is far more data than you can ever analyze. The idea is to turn that data into information and then turn that information into insight about your audience—and then use that wisdom to create a persuasive message.

We'll show you how to go about doing all this, with examples from business, government and nonprofits. We'll show you how to gather accurate data about your potential audiences and use that to begin segmenting them. We'll help you track their behaviors to see whether your programs have the desired effect. And we'll cover tools that are readily available, in some cases at no or low cost, and discuss when they should be used. To help you do all this we created a website—www.craftingpersuasion.com—which contains examples, exhibits, grids, and other tools to help you understand these concepts and craft your own communication strategies.

Behavioral Objective

If you are a _Star Wars_ fan, you are already familiar with Yoda's philosophical observation, "Do or not do. There is no try." In thinking about your communication strategy, changing attitudes or beliefs is necessary, but the heart of any campaign is what you want your target audience to do (or not do).

What behaviors do you want to influence? (Note: These behaviors may not always be the first thing you think about.) Can you quantify these actions, or the lack thereof? Is there a way to get your audience to repeat these desired behaviors without having to continuously commit all your resources?

Understanding how people make decisions and what influences them is critical to our process. The same strategy and messaging won't spur the same behavior in a factory line worker, a corporate middle manager, a senior executive and a retiree. Each has his or her own concerns. Each faces a different stage of life, with different responsibilities and different experiences. Even if you want to elicit the exact same behavior –voting for a given politician, for instance—these different audience members will not follow the exact same path to that decision.

If your challenge is to divert young people from becoming violent actors, do you try to reach them directly? Do you seek to enlist their religious advisers on your behalf? Do you have to start when they are very young? Do you appeal to values that are familiar to you or to them, or do you need to understand core values that people share across nations, cultures and faiths?

Consider efforts to convince the American public to support the United States Agency for International Development (USAID), the federal government's primary vehicle for delivering foreign aid. If you want to sway autoworkers in suburban Detroit, you might appeal to family values, since so much of this aid is humanitarian and aimed at helping women and children. You might try to reach them through their union leadership, their congressperson, or their pastor, rabbi or imam. But how do you discern the most effective approach? What do they care about? What is their attitude toward USAID and why?

This same thinking applies whether you are presenting a government policy, a new startup or an established consumer brand. You have to get into the heads of your audience. In Chapter 4, we'll explore different ways to craft a communication objective, including some examples of great ones, as well as how to create one for your own communication challenge.

Content

Once you have decided on your Audience and Behavioral Objective, the next critical part of your communication strategy is Content. This comprises the core of what we expect will persuade our audience, including everything from facts and figures to beliefs and perceptions. Effective content includes three critical components:

- **Benefit**—This is the promise you make to your target audience (i.e. what's in it for them if they change their behavior). We'll review various types of benefits, as well as the difference between primary and secondary benefits.

- **Reason to Believe (RTB)**—This involves *why* the audience should believe you can deliver on the promise. We'll explain different ways to accomplish this.

- **Tone and Character**—This is how you express your message. We'll show you ways to ensure the tone and character of your message stay consistent.

Here's why you need to take the time to *carefully* develop the content part of your communication strategy: Your strategy is all about choices— those few, critical choices—you need to make to deliver an attractive proposition for your target audience to consider (and ideally embrace). Not surprisingly, people are motivated to do things that benefit themselves. Some might do things for a higher cause, but even that benefits them, as it fulfills a personal need and value system. Without determining the key benefit your audience will derive from the behavior you seek to generate, you will have little success creating a persuasive message. This is, after all, the promise you make to your audience.

Next you have to convince them you can deliver on that promise. This is a huge challenge. Some people are more suspicious than others, but everyone is skeptical about something. All of us have been disappointed by broken promises. It is incumbent on you as a persuader to make your case, to prove to your audience that you can and will deliver on your promise.

Finally, the way your message "feels" has more impact on people than you might think. The tone or character of your communications can go a long way toward making your message come alive. Think about messages that had the greatest emotional impact on you, whether it was the crescendo of a great symphony, the passion of a great speaker or the finale of a great movie. Often, an audience is moved more by the feel of the message than the words and pictures used.

In Chapter 5, we take a deeper dive on these key content elements so you can see how they fit together. We'll share examples of how businesses,

NGOs and government agencies have successfully executed some brilliant communication campaigns based on a carefully constructed strategy, including content they successfully utilized.

Delivery

Delivering the message starts with translating the strategic words of the core content into a memorable and effective message. What words and visuals tell your story in a way that breaks through the noise, communicates your strategy and leaves an indelible impression on your audience?

In their book *The Underdog Advantage,* strategy consultants David Morey and Scott Miller write, "It is not enough to just pay attention to the details—you must make these details mean something, formed around one core communication strategy." Every detail in your communication either adds to or subtracts from your message. Your message is the sum of all the interactions your audience has with your promise—even elements over which you have no control.

For a consumer products marketer, delivering this message used to be relatively easy. You controlled the message that flowed to your audience. You knew the media environment—television, magazines, radio, newspapers and so forth. For the spokespersons of NGOs or the government, it was never so simple. They have always had their programs and press releases, but they can't control the domestic press or regional politician who might decide to go off script. It's imperative that we try to anticipate some of the wrenches people or circumstances will throw into our plans, and then proactively consider ways to mitigate the effects.

In developing your message, it's also critical to understand how your audience takes in and processes information:

- How does the audience think? What is relevant to them? When are they most receptive to new or different ideas?

- What are their existing associations? Where do our message, our desired behavioral changes and our beneficial promise fit in their world and among all the other decisions they face?

- Who influences their thinking? And who influences those influencers?

The next step is deciding *where* and *how* to deliver your message. As recently as the early 1990s this was a relatively simple undertaking, especially if you had a large budget. A marketing team typically spent most of its U.S. budget on television, especially the Big Three networks (ABC, NBC and CBS). You took the rest of your media budget and allocated it to the usual places: print, radio, billboards and other communication channels your media agency recommended.

Beginning in the mid-1990s, the internet dramatically changed all that. Most advertising in the United States now goes to online advertising, with Google and Facebook claiming 85 % of that channel. Newspapers and magazines have been in free fall the past twenty years. Radio has converted to subscription services, and now there are hundreds of television channels, not to mention the typically ad-free paid subscription channels, such as Netflix. Non-marketers and marketers alike must now choose from literally hundreds of online communication channels and platforms. Facebook. Instagram. Twitter. YouTube. The channels that are hot today could very well be cold tomorrow—remember AOL, Second Life and My Space?

This transformed media environment might actually help organizations with limited budgets, since they can target audiences more precisely and the cost of online production has fallen dramatically lower than the cost of network television commercial production. Knowing which channels and platforms to pick—and why—should not be a game of chance. Chapter 6 will give you an overview of the ways to deliver your messages, as well as the different communication channels available to you and how to select the right ones for your communication strategy and campaigns.

Evaluation

The popular maxim, "That which gets measured gets done," couldn't be truer. It's critical to agree on what success looks like before you begin *any* communication campaign. Otherwise, you run the risk of engaging in an ongoing, often emotional debate with the rest of your team (as well as your management) on whether your communication campaign accomplished what you set out to do. Take it from the authors—these are conversations you do not want to have.

With the growth of various digital channels, there are more new and powerful ways of measuring the impact of your communication efforts than ever before: clicks, views, likes, recommendations, sentiment analysis. And most critical of all, these same channels can provide a more direct view of audience action. Whether you are evaluating e-commerce buys or the overall tone of the reactions to a campaign, digital channels can show whether the audience tracks or avoids the actions you defined as your Behavioral Objective.

Importantly, having a well thought out strategy with buy-in from the organization can help you respond more quickly to unexpected changes and unanticipated events. An established strategy allows you and your organization to make decisions about urgent actions within a context that has been thoughtfully considered, rather than on an ad hoc basis.

Chapter 7 provides a broad view of various ways to gather and analyze data to evaluate how well you are implementing your communication strategy. We'll bring you up to date on some exciting technology developments that offer excellent ways to share your evaluation and analysis with the key stakeholders in your communication efforts. Chapter 8 goes deeper into how to deal with the significant challenges of persuading various types of audiences, especially ones not easily swayed (since it's a pretty good bet you will have to persuade your future audiences the old-fashioned way—by working hard to earn it). Chapter 9 is a deep dive on how to do a better job connecting and communicating effectively with youth, which might be especially valuable for readers no longer in that demographic. Chapter 10 provides an overview on the ever-changing landscape of digital marketing and provides perspective on how to keep the right balance between developing an effective communication strategy and figuring out the most efficient and effective way to implement it.

One of the most valuable chapters in this book might be Chapter 11, which outlines best practices on dealing with the most time critical area of communication strategy—better known as "issues management." If you've ever been in a PR crisis, you already know what we're talking about (and if you haven't, now is the time to learn what you need to know in advance). Chapter 12 and 13 provide a series of real world case studies from the business and non-profit world to show why you need to implement the ABCDE Communication Model. Chapter 14 recaps common pitfalls to avoid in developing and implementing your communication strategy. We wrap up the book in Chapter 15 with a look ahead at what to expect in terms of communication and all the ways it can be executed and evaluated in a rapidly changing world.

At the end of the chapters, we've also included a brief article from a guest writer that provides valuable perspective on a wide variety of communication topics we discuss in the book. Many of these writers have also served on the faculty of the Marketing College, and we appreciate their contributions both in and out of the classroom.

Let's get started

Before we dive into the details, we wanted to provide a summary of the ABCDE Communication Model, along with definitions for each part of it. (See Figure 2.1) We will use this format throughout the book as we share various case studies and examples with you. We also have a downloadable version you can use to help guide your own strategy work.

⬇ Online Exhibit 2.1

FIGURE 2.1 **The ABCDE Communication Model Grid** *(with definitions)*	
Audience	Who you are trying to persuade (defined by demographics, behavior, attitudes, psychographics, etc.)?
• Audience Insight	Based on consumer research and analysis, what do you already know about your target audience that will be helpful in creating a persuasive communication campaign?
Behavioral Objectives	What exactly do you want your target audience to do based on this communication campaign?

Content	
• Benefit	What are you promising your target audience will get in return for the behavior you are advocating? Bottom-line, what's in it for them (especially from an emotional POV)?
• Reason to Believe	Why should the target audience believe you can deliver the benefit you have promised them (i.e. endorsement, mechanism of action, ingredients, product/service attributes, etc.)?
• Tone/Character	What is the personality, attitude and look/feel of your message (expressed in three words or less)?
Delivery—Media	Which online and offline media channels are you going to use to get your message out (e.g., Facebook ads, YouTube videos, print ads, PR campaign, TV commercials, etc.)?
Delivery—Message	What's the overall message you are going to be delivering to your target audience?
• On Brand	How does this communication campaign tie into and leverage your overall brand image?
• Recognizable	What is in this campaign that will make it easy for your target audience to quickly identify it with your brand?
• Simple	Is your overall message clear and simple enough that the target audience will be able to understand it quickly and easily?
• Attention Grabbing	What will be included in your communication campaign that will get the attention of your target audience?
Evaluation	What metrics are you going to use to evaluate the overall success of this communication campaign? Over what time period?

While this model was developed and optimized during the development of the Marketing College for the benefit of a U.S. government audience, the model works the same for businesses, nonprofits, NGOs and startups. We hope you enjoy learning about the ABCDE Communication Model as much as we've enjoyed developing and teaching it over the past 10 years.

Check out the Crafting Persuasion website where the online exhibits are located!

Throughout this book, we will be referring to various online exhibits (⬇ Online Exhibit) to show you real world communication examples of what we will be explaining. In addition, you will also find helpful tools for your own use (such as a downloadable version of the ABCDE Communication Model). The website is **www.CraftingPersuasion.com** and is free for anyone to use (readers and non-readers alike). The website is organized to make it easy to find the online exhibits referred to in the upcoming chapters.

Over time, we will be adding and updating more real world examples on this website. We would welcome your suggestions on what we should include.

You can reach us at info@craftingpersuasion.com. We look forward to hearing from you!

Don't Underestimate the Power of the ABCDE Model

Dave Wallinga
VP of Marketing, Panda Restaurant Group

In a world in which we place extreme value on things we may not understand (think: emerging technology, modern art), it is easy to place less value on—or even dismiss—something we immediately and intuitively *get*.

Any time an article, book, podcast or webinar is titled "The ABCs of…" or "Five Steps to…", it signals that we're about to learn an approach that is inherently simple. Spoiler alert: The ABCDE Model is simple in theory and structure, but mastering it is anything but, and the results you can generate through its use can be world-changing.

In the visual arts and music, minimalism is an attempt to explore the essential elements of an art form. Emerging in the late 1950s, works such as Frank Stella's *Black Paintings* influenced a new school of artists, including Donald Judd and Robert Morris, and served as the precursor to a branch of modern classical music created by composers such as Steve Reich and Philip Glass. Minimal art (also called ABC art!) is the creative culmination of reductionist tendencies.

Minimalism as a current social phenomenon is about ridding your life of unnecessary material possessions—or decluttering—so you can focus on what's more important, such as experiences or relationships with loved ones and friends.

Think of the ABCDE Communication Model as a means of strategic decluttering that creates focus and clarity to make your communications more powerful.

By building your communications plan around a single, clearly defined target audience, the odds of reaching the people you need to increase many times over. This may or may not come at the expense of reaching others with your message. However, the more complex your communications challenge, the more critical it is to chip away at it one clearly defined target audience at a time.

You don't need to become an expert in human behavior to understand your target audience, although the desire to master A (never mind B, C, D and E) has launched a wide range of fields, including psychology, anthropology, sociology, market research, user-experience design and design thinking. Enlisting the help of experts in these disciplines and professions may be of tremendous value when the scope of your work calls for such assistance. A simple, thoughtful approach may also suffice.

Journalism schools teach students to write stories with the reader, viewer, or listener in mind. Similarly, before you start your first draft, you simply need to identify whom you're trying to reach, influence, or sell to. Then, follow the steps in this book and work the ABCDE Model. It works because of its focus, clarity, and simplicity. ∎

CHAPTER 3

'A' Is for Audience

"The odds of hitting your target go up dramatically when you aim at it."

–Mal Pancoast (President, The Breakthrough Coach)

From that very first meeting at the White House, Dr. Jim Nyce has been a part of the USMCC faculty. He is our expert on marketing audience research and consumer insights. He has led global market research teams at Kraft, GFK and Sun Products, and he brings the depth and breadth of his expertise to our students. (You can find some of his thoughts on consumer research in the sidebar at the end of this chapter.)

According to Dr. Nyce, one major mistake when thinking about a target audience is to make assumptions. This is especially true when it comes to understanding what really motivates your audience. History is littered with marketers and advertising teams who thought they knew their audience when they really didn't. Too often we assume we know our audience because "they are just like us." This is such a persistent issue that one advertising agency had T-shirts printed for their entire employee team that read, in bold letters: "YOU ARE NOT THE TARGET CUSTOMER."

So, let's put this challenge to the test. Without cheating and looking up answers on Google, let's see how much you really know about Americans. (We put the answers at the end of the chapter.)

1. According to the Census Bureau's American Community Survey, what percentage of U.S. households "speak a language other than English" at home?

2. Between 2007 and 2016, the unauthorized immigrant population in the United States:

   a. Increased about 26 %
   b. Increased about 12 %
   c. Decreased about 4 %
   d. Decreased about 13 %

3. As of 2017, what percentage of Americans had a passport? (Bonus points: What proportion had one in the late 1980s?)

4. What percentage of American households make less than $50,000 per year?

5. According to the Pew Research Center, what percentage of American households include "a married couple raising their own children?"

6. In 2014, what percentage of births were to unmarried mothers? (Bonus points: What was the proportion in 1960?)

7. What percentage of Americans have graduated from college with a bachelor's degree?

8. What percentage of Asian Americans have graduated from college with a bachelor's degree?

9. What percentage of American households carry credit card debt?

10. What percentage of Americans by age group say they "often" get their news from a print newspaper (18 to 29 years old; 30 to 49; 50 to 64; and 65-plus)?

11. What percentage of American adults believe that human beings evolved through natural processes over millions of years without divine intervention?

We'd bet that some of these questions—probably even most of them—threw you for a loop. Conventional wisdom, popular conversation and the assumptions we make often don't match the reality of the people we hope to reach and thought we knew. How do you think you would do with the consumers you know far less well? Even if you're part of a given target audience, can you truly speak for the diversity of the entire group?

Research, research, research

Consumer research provides the foundation for any effective message, and all the elements of the communications process can be evaluated—the audience definition, the behavioral objective, the content strategy, message development, media selection and effectiveness. You should be skeptical of anyone who skimps on research and suggests they "know the audience" based on their personal experience and interactions. If they don't have reliably generated consumer research data, call it what it is: total BS. We can't stress this enough. If you make the wrong initial assertions about your target audience, the rest of the ABCDE communication model has almost no shot at success.

In this chapter, we will discuss two aspects of audience analysis. The first is how to gather the data. The second is how to turn that data into consumer insights—the truths about the world (at least from the perspective of your target audience) that create an opportunity for your organization to achieve its goals and deliver a benefit. Both the gathering data and turning it into insight steps begin with an understanding of the current attitudes and behavior of your target audience (i.e., the segment of the population whose attitudes and behavior you hope to influence). Rather than relying on assumptions, we should dig deep to understand how they think, feel, and behave.

You don't need to be an expert in consumer marketing research to do this—and we're not trying to make you one. While there are dedicated professionals who do this for a living, an abundance of data and resources are available if you have the determination and take the time to better understand your target audience.

What's the goal?

Before you start to plan and conduct *any* market research, you need to consider two key questions. First, decide on your objectives. Bottom line, what are you trying to find out from whom? By starting with a clear objective, you can determine the best research approach and tools you need to use (and, if needed, secure the appropriate resources and professional assistance). In addition, clearly stated research objectives will provide important perspective for your team and boss about what the proposed research will and won't be able to address.

The second question to ask before starting any consumer research is what business decision(s) you are going to make based on your findings. Remember, consumer research is a tool and a process. It doesn't give you all the answers, and it certainly does not make decisions. Consumer research only provides guidance, but without it you don't have a basis for well-informed decisions. If you are not planning on making a key decision based on the research you're about to invest in, you are wasting your organization's time and money. Trusting your gut might occasionally work in Vegas, but it's no way to understand your target consumer. You learn to understand your audience by collecting and analyzing *qualitative and quantitative research* about them. Let's make sure you understand the difference between the two and when to use each.

Qualitative research

Qualitative research helps develop initial hypotheses about how your target consumers think and feel about key issues. This is generally done by asking individuals or small groups questions and carefully assessing their responses. Deciding to enter the already crowded household cleaning products category might seem crazy, but that's what two roommates, Adam Lowry and Eric Ryan, set out to do in 2000 when they created their company Method. Through an ongoing series of interviews and discussions with consumers, they found many consumers had serious concerns about the ingredients in their cleaning products, as well as the impact those ingredients might have on their bodies and the environment. Based in part on their initial qualitative research, they went on to launch what became one of the fastest growing private companies in the U.S. until Ecover acquired it in 2012.

The sorts of qualitative research techniques Lowry and Ryan used allow you to probe issues and answers in a way that gets past the top-line responses of your audience. What do they like and why? What don't they like and why not? What led them to that particular attitude or behavior? To whom do they listen? To whom do they give advice? Why do they do that? A well-crafted line of qualitative inquiry can help solicit individuals to express themselves more fully than might be possible in a quantitative survey. (See Box 3.1)

BOX 3.1
Tips for guiding and observing quantitative research discussions

For the discussion guide

Most of the qualitative methods require a professional moderator and a discussion guide, which is developed between the client and the moderator to ensure that the critical topics are covered and, importantly, to stipulate the order in which they should be addressed. The objectives include the desire to have a natural flow of the topics and questions to make the respondents comfortable. A natural discussion is much better than a perceived interrogation.

The guide moves from the general to the specific to establish a context for the later questions. Often moderators will allow the early discussion to be spontaneous, so they can uncover unanticipated lines of thought and discussion. If the discussion does not get to all the points desired, a more-directed discussion ensues.

Often in communication groups, people are shown examples of a program or campaign idea to get their reactions. Assuming there are multiple groups, the moderator will rotate the order of the examples being shown to avoid an order bias with the stimuli.

(continues on next page)

(Box 3.1 continued)

For the observer

When observing qualitative research, three things are essential:

- Maintain an attitude of openness and respect even if you are observing from another room. Try to see the world from your participants' points of view. That is why you have recruited them.

- Be open to what you don't like hearing. Listen for thinking that is counter to your own. Listen for the unexpected. This is all input for your benefit.

- Don't judge. Participants always have valuable wisdom and insights to share, but only if you are willing to listen and hear it.

However, *qualitative* research cannot provide a substitute for *quantitative* research. (See Box 3.2) Doing more and more focus groups and interviews does not make them quantitative. They are not representative of a larger audience because, by and large, qualitative research is conducted with a small, unrepresentative sample of your broader target. What this research can do is provide you with hypotheses you can then test quantitatively. It can help you uncover topics, issues and attitudes you might not have discovered on your own and might otherwise have failed to include in your quantitative study. In this regard, qualitative techniques are critical tools.

BOX 3.2
The capabilities and limits of qualitative research

What qualitative research can do:
- Tap the creativity of the target
- Help penetrate rationalized or superficial responses
- Provide depth of understanding
- Allow for open, flexible and dynamic input from the target
- Provide a rich source of ideas for communications developers

What it cannot do:
- Provide comparable measures against standards or across time
- Be projected onto a larger population
- Reliably predict the responses of a broad range of the target audience

There are a variety of qualitative research techniques available, including focus groups, in-depth interviews, and ethnographies. Let's explore each of them and learn their relative strengths and weaknesses.

Focus groups

A focus group, the most commonly used qualitative technique, is a structured discussion led by a trained moderator. It is important to use a trained moderator to get the most out of these sessions and make sure all participants are heard. A professional moderator will be able to guide the group through a preplanned discussion and to probe new and unexpected threads of discussion that come up in the conversation.

Typically, a group includes five to ten people, selected based on the topic of the research. Depending on the nature of the conversation, you will seek to compose these groups with representatives of various demographic segments, such as age, income, location and gender. For sensitive issues or with certain cultures, individual groups might be limited to one gender. We usually conduct three to six groups to cover a given topic. Each group can take one to two hours and is generally conducted at a neutral site with an audience of interested parties watching and listening in an adjacent room.

Focus groups operate in a relatively standard way, although individual moderators' techniques vary. Prior to the sessions, the client that is requesting the research will provide a discussion guide that walks through the key topics to be covered. This information is reviewed with the moderator, who can provide guidance on the order of the questions and learn more about areas the client would like to have probed.

If the topic is sensitive and very personal, it may take a series of questions to get the individuals in the group to open up in front of strangers. For example, asking young women about their personal hygiene preferences and decisions could result in a very quiet room. A good moderator can sometimes break down these barriers and get people to talk.

Often, though, the initial responses are going to be very basic and not very helpful. The moderator will want to know if the client wants these answers probed further. If so, the moderator can ask indirect questions that might get the individuals to open up about their personal experiences, who provided guidance, and how they decided which products to use.

These indirect-questioning techniques often work better, for example, when asking women in male-dominated cultures about their views on important and sensitive issues. Women who would never volunteer an opinion in an open or mixed setting might feel comfortable enough in a single-sex group to discuss their views—and even then, good moderators might need to rely on subtler, less-direct questions to gain deeper insights.

Strengths of focus groups Focus groups are low cost, especially relative to other traditional techniques, and the interactions that develop in a roomful of people can lead to a whole that's greater than the sum of its parts. Often, as people hear others open up, they feel freer to offer their own opinion. A skilled moderator can tell if people are just parroting the points of view of a dominant member and then dig deeper to elicit other views. In the most valuable sessions, respondents build on the ideas of others in the room or may take the discussion in a totally unexpected direction.

These sessions allow the client to hear how the participants speak about a given topic. What words do they use? In what context? How do they feel about the topic and why? One of our faculty, while working on a bar soap product with a very powerful perfume as a distinguishing feature, conducted a focus group about the brand before it was launched. The team had envisioned a marketing campaign that showed the product being used in a crashing surf with young actors and high energy. But one of the respondents said, "I think it would wake me up in the morning," and the brand took its marketing campaign in an entirely different direction. They landed on a television commercial that featured actors starting to lather up in the shower and, as they caught a whiff of the soap, looking instantly invigorated.

Focus groups also provide a chance for marketers to dig further into the respondents' wants, needs and attitudes. What do they believe about a given subject, issue or controversy? Why do they believe what they believe? Who influences their beliefs? How deeply are they held? Have they considered an alternative approach? To ask these questions in a quantitative study would require a large number of open-ended questions and still would not allow for immediate follow-up in response to individual answers.

This ability to probe allows the client to develop new hypotheses that can then be tested empirically. Whether it is a totally new approach to the communication plan or an entirely new direction for the project, the results from these groups can provide the grist for further discussion and, ultimately, for quantitative questioning.

Weaknesses of focus groups The strengths of focus groups can also be a liability. Group dynamics, if not managed well by the moderator, can result in group think. Some people are just talkers. They want to dominate the conversation, and the result is either that others don't talk or that they just agree with the alpha dog. A good moderator can nip this in the bud. In some cases, the individual can be politely removed from the group. Conversely, sometimes even the most-skilled moderators cannot get a group to open up. Some sensitive topics are not appropriate for a group discussion, and taboo topics such as honor killings or situations in which respondents feel threatened if they speak might require alternative approaches.

But the biggest weakness of focus groups, like any qualitative techniques, is that they are not representative of a larger audience. One of our faculty worked with a Fortune 100 corporation that proudly told him that they had conducted 1,000 focus groups. What an incredible waste. They had spent the time and money to hold three to six groups in cities all over the world, and they still didn't have quantitative data upon which to base key decisions.

In-depth interviews

In-depth interviews, typically conducted one-on-one by an experienced moderator trained in this specific format, can address some of the problems found in focus group settings. These interviews can occur at neutral sites with viewing and listening capabilities, or even in a private home with a recording. Generally, you should plan to conduct interviews with eight to ten respondents to fully cover an issue. Interviews run 45 to 90 minutes and, if stacked back to back, they can be exhausting for the moderator and clients who are viewing the proceedings from a nearby room.

Strengths of in-depth interviews This technique is especially useful for sensitive issues or for topics about which participants may be easily influenced in a group setting. Topics that a respondent simply won't discuss in public can often be addressed in this setting, especially if the moderator is skilled at making the respondent comfortable.

In-depth interviews are also good for picking the brains of powerful or uniquely qualified individuals. For example, one pharmaceutical company's project involved discussing a new drug with cardiologists. Not only was it difficult to get these doctors to organize their schedules for a group session, but prior experience suggested that their self-image would not allow them to open up about their views, experiences and decision-making in front of their peers. Similarly, discussions with religious leaders in a highly charged and potentially dangerous location might require one-on-one interviews.

As with focus groups, speaking with individuals allows us to see how they talk about given subjects. What terms do they use? How energized are they about the subject? What other topics and individuals do they associate with a given subject? This last point is important. How are concepts connected? These are what we call benefit ladders or decision trees. One benefit relates to or grows out of another, higher benefit, which grows out of another, even higher benefit. As we move up this benefit ladder, we hope to discover the root of the respondent's thinking and beliefs.

Weaknesses of in-depth interviews There are times when, even after careful screening to select the respondents, you will end up with some people who simply aren't talkative. They might not be particularly interested in your topic, or it might make them uncomfortable. In addition, these interviews are time consuming. You can get to perhaps 30 people in three focus groups over five or six hours, but one-on-one interviews will take two or three times as long to get the opinions of ten.

Don't just hear what you want to hear

Your job as the client is to lay out the discussion guide for your moderator and then *listen*. The people who observe these groups or interviews too often try to get evidence to support a point of view they already have. This is a waste. If you have made up your mind, why are you spending the time and money to do research?

Of course, you will probably hear responses that support your hypothesis. After all, you're a smart person with a great deal of knowledge about the topic you're researching. But that is not the purpose of this work. You need to listen for the exceptions. You need to listen for the people who disagree with you and who don't like what you are saying or doing. You need to listen for their underlying reasoning. You can certainly build on the positives you hear, but understanding the concerns and objections of the people you are trying to sway is the real value.

Ethnographies

People don't always know why or how they do things. They don't always think about the steps they take in a process they've been doing for years. They don't always recall where they get their information or to whom they listen. In such situations, ethnographic research can prove quite valuable.

This technique has its roots in anthropology, in which experts hoped that, through observation, they could discern the habits of different cultures and societies and, by extension, form hypotheses about their thinking. In current ethnographic practice, anthropologists worry that their mere presence can change the natural behavior of the animals or people they are studying. In marketing pursuits, however, we observe subjects in a different way, generally asking them to perform a particular action (whereas an anthropologist would merely observe for weeks at a time to discern emerging patterns).

Using our version of ethnographies, we engage in a prearranged opportunity to observe and talk to people in their own environments—their home, on the job, etc. The focus is generally on one individual, although interactions with family, peers and others may be important elements, as well. The approach is far more flexible than the scientifically bound anthropological methods. Usually, a company will conduct eight to twelve interviews to cover a variety of perspectives on a topic. It can be helpful to have a moderator or even an anthropologist on your team, but generally your communications team will conduct the observations firsthand. In this technique, the observers are not behind a mirror or in another room. They are in the room with the respondent.

To give an example, one of our faculty was leading a team developing Mexican food products for the general market. As it happened, none of his team at the time was Hispanic (an oversight he later remedied). Recognizing that the team had no firsthand experience in preparing Mexican dishes, he organized an ethnographic study. He paired a client team member with one of his ad agency team, and each was given a translator. Their research partner recruited a dozen women who were willing to allow these outsiders into their homes as they prepared their families' favorite meals. The company paid for all the ingredients as well as a stipend for their time.

One of the women was making a meal that included refried beans, a staple of the cuisine. As she cooked, the team asked her questions. She had done this so many times, she didn't even realize some of the things she was doing. It was just cooking the way her mother had taught her.

Now, in making refried beans you start with dried beans that are soaked overnight to soften them. The team noted that when she drained the beans, she kept the water instead of pouring it down the drain. When asked why, she said that was just what she always did. But later, after the beans were cooked and mashed, she used that saved water to create the consistency she wanted in her final product. Had she been asked in a normal interview how she made refried beans, it is unlikely she would have noted that she reused the water she had saved from soaking the beans. It wasn't something the team had heard before.

In a factory setting, the soaking water is disposed of when the beans are drained. The cooked and mashed beans are thinned with fresh water. The product development team quickly realized how much of the flavor and nutrients that were captured in the soaking water were lost in the normal factory process. Without observing this woman, the team might never have made that critical connection, which led to dramatic improvements in consumer acceptance of the new bean products.

Strengths and weaknesses of Ethnographies Like a one-on-one interview, this technique allows for a deep dive into the respondent's behavior, but with the added benefit of observing actions and inputs they might not otherwise mention because they have so thoroughly internalized them. Participants might assume that their actions are common to everyone, so there's no point in bringing them up. They may assume that the moderators and interviewers know things that those individuals don't actually know. If other family members are involved, their inputs and reactions can also be probed in context. This method gives the researcher the opportunity to discover the unexpected and unanticipated. However, individuals or single families can only speak for themselves, and it takes more time and money to conduct a single ethnographic case study—let alone enough of them to get a range of in-depth experiences. And if your interest does not relate to an activity that your target audience regularly performs, this tool might not provide much help.

Online or Mobile Ethnographies As with traditional ethnographies, online or mobile approaches provide an avenue through which a marketing team can talk to and obtain input from respondents in their own environment, whether that is at home, work, internet cafe, etc. In this case, the respondents write blogs, take and upload pictures or video, and answer questions interactively. The tool is less expensive while remaining flexible— perhaps even more flexible than traditional onsite ethnographies. Eight to twelve of these types of interviews can provide rich, multimedia output that can be useful to share with others on the team. But it does require daily oversight by a trained anthropologist or moderator, as the respondents are often providing this input at their own pace and in their own time.

Quantitative Research

Unlike qualitative research, quantitative research is all about measurement. It uses large samples of your target audience to provide a comparison with historical benchmarks and to allow for a projection of the results to a wider universe. "Custom" quantitative research, also known as "primary" or "ad hoc" research, has the following attributes:

- It's conducted at a given point in time
- It addresses a particular communications issue
- It can be replicated
- It can be projected to a larger target population *if done correctly*

By definition, custom studies have no set design, although it's often wise to rely on proven approaches and techniques. As noted, these studies typically require large sample sizes to allow for rigorous, statistically significant analysis among identified subgroups. These studies can be executed via the internet, mobile phones and more traditional in-market intercept methods. All are viable data collection approaches, depending on the local conditions. It is best to engage with a proven research partner to guide you through research design and execution for your objectives.

As with qualitative research, there are a variety of quantitative research methods you can deploy, including segmentation studies, attitude and behavior studies, tracking studies, and communication pre-testing. Let's explore them and learn when each would be most appropriate.

Segmentation studies

The primary purpose of a segmentation study is to identify and quantify various target groups and subgroups based on common beliefs, attitudes, needs and behaviors within a given market. Segments are usually based on attitudes, but they can predict or be based on associations with certain behaviors, as well. Ultimately, we are trying to identify communication opportunities for both individual segments as well as the common or shared opportunities across combinations of segments. Ideally, you will conduct some qualitative work first, and use it to help develop the hypotheses and alternatives you should include in your quantitative research design.

Attitude and behavior studies

Sometimes called "usage and attitude studies" or "habits and practices studies," these surveys quantify the attitudes, habits and behaviors of the target audience. In the commercial world, we might want to understand the personal grooming habits of men versus women, or across age groups or cultures or races. Digging deeper, we might want to understand the attitudes and/or beliefs that might impact these behaviors. For example, in the nonprofit world, the kernel of what we want to understand might relate to an individual's willingness to donate—or more broadly, the donation history of a segment of people along with an understanding of the considerations that led different individuals or subsets to make the donation or pass on it. Similarly, to counter violent extremism, we have spent years trying to understand the range of motivations that have led individuals to turn to violence across the globe and the entire political spectrum.

Attitude and behavior studies are intended to delve beyond the surface level, easily observable attitudes and beliefs and understand the roots from which they grow. They can also be very effective in identifying developing patterns or shifts in behavior that might require strategic redirection. Ultimately, these studies can allow us to understand and compare our own beliefs, images, messages and attitudes with those of our targets, and various target segments to one another.

Tracking studies

Let's say you just took over as head of marketing for the local Turkey Trot race, which is held each Thanksgiving to raise money for local charities. As you plan your marketing activities for next year's event, it would help to have several years of survey research that tracks the overall awareness of, regard for, and attitudes about the event. By asking the same questions every year, you could compare data over time and identify. The information and the trends it reveals can be extremely valuable in determining how you want to focus your marketing efforts, revealing ways you can improve your outreach

Such tracking studies deliver insights into changes in attitudes, beliefs, and behaviors over time. As such, they provide some of the most valuable types of quantitative research you can get, because the findings are so highly actionable. However, to accomplish this, each study needs to remain virtually identical to its predecessors. Changing questions, while timely for an ad hoc study, can make the study unusable for tracking purposes.

Tracking studies can be used to assess the impact of changes in communications programs, the introduction of new programs or the cessation of past programs. You can monitor changes in attitudes, opinions and behavior—potentially in ways that provide a deeper understanding of the cause and effect. Importantly, these studies can measure the impact not only of our efforts, but those of other actors. Similar to attitude studies, tracking studies can identify patterns in attitudes and related behaviors, including shifts that might require a response from you and your team.

Communication pre-testing

This is a very specific type of quantitative testing. Given the high cost of some types of marketing and media production, especially television

commercials, most private-sector marketing organizations test their communication executions throughout each stage of the development process.
Companies generally have a consistent set of testing methodologies that all
their executions must pass through, so they can compare the performance
of each stage with the final marketplace results and develop benchmarks
for future communications projects.

The objective is to use techniques that best predict marketplace success, of course. Most tools expose the executions to actual target audiences
to determine whether they understand the messaging and are moved to
action by it. Most of the tools also provide some diagnostic insight as to
whether or not the communication worked with the particular audience.
Did the communication attract their attention? Did they even remember
they saw it? Did they understand the promise and the benefit? Did they
like the communication? Did it change their attitude toward the subject?
Will it lead to the desired behavior? There is a continuum of questions,
with the latter becoming less precise and predictive.

A variety of low-cost tools are available to test ideas at an early concept
stage. And other affordable tests can provide insight into effectiveness of
an evolving plan before major investments are made. With the growth of
communication platforms such as YouTube, one can create, execute and
test finished-looking messages for very little money relative to historic
television advertising expenses. And because a TV commercial can run
into seven figures on production costs alone, pre-testing is all but essential
before making a final decision to proceed.

Ways of collecting quantitative data

When quantitative market research as we know it got its start, roughly a
century ago, most of it was done in person. In a model that held up for
decades, an interviewer would meet face-to-face with the subject. There
was a time, not all that long ago, when a researcher would knock on your
door and seek permission to ask you questions.

Another popular option was the "mall intercept," where you would be
walking through a shopping mall and a person with a clipboard would ask
you if you had time to do a research survey. Sometimes they would do the
interview right there where you stood, while other times they would bring

you to a separate room in the mall, especially if they wanted you to sample a product or watch a commercial and comment. An alternative to that method was to contact you in advance and ask you to come to a given location to participate in a study. As the expense of long-distance calls decreased and the cost and hassles of in-person interviews grew more problematic, phone or mailed interviews became the norm. In some cases, a subject might get a diary with instructions to track certain habits and practices.

Today, quantitative research runs through three primary channels: in person (which remains very effective); on the internet; and by phone or mobile phone. There are pluses and minuses to each. These studies can be expensive, so you want to make sure you get a representative sample of your target audience. When using the lower-cost methodologies, getting a sample of the right nature and composition is critical. Some of these tools can be either very good or very bad, depending on the quality and size of the sample.

In Person

The intercept method or the so-called central location test both remain viable. By finding a location with a great deal of traffic and then managing the respondents so you get the cross-section you need, you can obtain substantial value for your research dollar. Central location testing can help solve the sampling challenges if you utilize a reputable local firm that has a track record of providing statistically valid, representative samples. The studies themselves can be executed in a church basement, a school, a social club or similar venues.

Internet

This is becoming a much more widely used methodology. Depending on the country, services can help you gather the appropriate sample, and then you can execute the survey rather efficiently. Tools like SurveyMonkey can be useful as long as you are confident about the quality of the sample. When the client doesn't have strict control over who is in the sample, surveys can mislead and might be worse than no research at all. Fortunately, most of the established online survey companies offer tools and services that help ensure an effective sample group.

More and more the internet methodology is being executed on smartphones rather than computers. If you are using a smartphone questionnaire to gather information, you need to consider the length and number of questions, as well as any stimulus you try to use to engage respondents. For example, if you are trying to show someone a photo or a poster to get their response, keep in mind how small those items look on a phone screen. It might impact your results.

Telephone and mobile

Oral interviews done on a landline or a mobile phone can be useful, if respondents can easily hear and understand the interviewer. Native-language speakers are desirable. Interviewers who have learned the language and have heavy accents can be difficult to understand, or even invite respondents to suspect that they are being interrogated by a foreign actor. In many parts of the world, mobile phone interviews using live interviewers rather than smartphones might be the primary vehicle to gather your data.

The market research cycle

Good market research doesn't end. You do it at the outset of a marketing campaign to understand your audience and generate insights, starting with qualitative techniques to probe and generate hypotheses and then flesh out those ideas with quantitative techniques. Even before you launch your campaign, you can employ tracking studies to look for emerging patterns, identify anomalies and anticipate behavioral changes. Once you have developed your communications plans, you can use quantitative testing to evaluate alternative approaches, executions, strategies and audiences. The quantitative techniques discussed in this chapter provide insights across each of these tasks.

Before the strategic work is underway, you and your management team will need to make a critical decision about what you need to measure to determine the effectiveness of the project. You must reach a consensus on these metrics before you execute the program, because looking for metrics after the fact will never elicit the same level of confidence in the people judging the performance. Furthermore, by challenging the metrics you choose, you can ensure that you can, in fact, measure anything meaningful.

If you can't determine how to measure performance, you should seriously ask yourself whether the program is worthwhile.

Ultimately, you need to measure the performance of your programs—and ideally understand all the key elements of success or failure—so you can improve the next round of efforts. From there the cycle begins again. (Box 3.3)

BOX 3.3
The Target Audience Research Cycle

- Know **who** you want to talk to (your target)

- Know **what** you want to communicate (clear objectives)

- Learn **how** to make your message meaningful to them (use research to drive data, turn data into information and information into insights)

- **Pretest** your communication messages before you field them

- **Track** your target's understanding of your messaging and the effectiveness of your efforts

- Build and preserve your **institutional memory** about your target, their understanding and their behaviors.

Generating insights

Once you plant a stake in the ground about your audience, it is imperative to turn the data you have gathered about each group into information—and subsequently into insights. An insight explains a common habit, belief, practice or attitude that your target exhibits relative to the behavior in question. For example, if asked to market a laundry product to a particular audience, you would want these key insights:

- **Habits**—How do they separate their washing loads? How much time do they devote to laundry? How many people are they doing laundry for? These insights would help you determine whether the behavior you want to affect is consistent or at odds with their normal habits.

- **Beliefs**—Which brands do they trust and why? Did mom teach them what to use and they never found a reason to change? You can't know how to change their minds if you don't know how they think.

- **Practices**—What are the processes they use with their laundry? Are they diligent about the temperatures they use for different fabrics or colors? Do they pretreat spots on their clothes? Do they use a fabric softener in the rinse cycle or in the dryer?

- **Attitudes**—How important is doing laundry to this person? Is it something they are proud of as a service to their family? Is it just a chore that they want to get finished as soon as possible?

Now take these same four questions into your world. If you are trying to convince a group of people to walk away from violence against an ethnic group, you want to understand whether their actions are an ingrained habit within their peer group. You want to know what beliefs they hold about that given group, where those beliefs originated, and why they still hold those attitudes. Such insights are essential in helping us to ground our messages in a "truth" or a "real-life" experience for the people we want to reach. They help your target audience relate to your message. (See Box 3.4)

BOX 3.4
Engaging with a Target Audience

Good communication doesn't preach to its targets; it engages with them. It starts from their perspective and influences. The point is to have the audience believe, "You understand me." Consider a classic set of commercials developed by the U.S. Marine Corps in the late 1990s. (⬇ **Online Exhibit 3.1**) In them, young men battle through mazes and barriers that look more like video games than anything you'd encounter in real life. Having traversed all the obstacles, the protagonist pulls a saber from an orb, only to have a knight or monster rise to challenge them. He defeats his foe, raises his saber and is struck by an electrical bolt that transforms him into a Marine in full dress uniform.

Now, guess the audience insight that led to this commercial concept. In this case, the critical insight emerged from the habits of the Marine Corps' target audience. Many young men of prime recruitment age are avid video gamers and seek adventure and excitement in their virtual worlds. The commercials aligned with that desire.

But remember, insights come from you and your analysis of the audience, not directly from the audience. While based on an in-depth understanding of information from multiple sources, you need to make the connections. So beyond solely looking at the habits, beliefs, practices and attitudes of your audience, look for other sources of consumer insight. For example, competitors often provide a wellspring of insight. Can you identify a negative about your competitor that your audience recognizes and dislikes? You might not want to talk about their negatives directly—after all, you don't want to give them any more exposure than they already have—but you can talk about the positives of your product or service. For example, generations of consumers used Listerine, believing that terrible taste must be killing some germs, right? But then Scope started talking about the same germ-killing benefits with a pleasant taste, instead. The insight? Consumers wanted the benefit without the pain.

The bottom line is that the insight step is the difference between communication that is simply on strategy and communication that is truly persuasive. Insights can uncover unmet or unarticulated needs of the audience. They can increase the relevance of your messages. And they create a bond between your message and your audience by establishing a connection between your brand and the life of the target audience. As you craft your content strategy, spend time to understand how your audience insights fit within it.

How P&G used consumer insights to become a category leader

A real-world example helps to illustrate the power of gleaning consumer insights as part of your communication planning. When it's done right, fortunes can be made and former category leaders can be pushed aside.

Ever since its founding in 1837, P&G has been a strong believer in listening and responding to its consumers. You may have heard the story that Ivory Soap was created accidently, when P&G received letters from consumers across America asking for more of "that soap that floats," since this quality made it easy to find the soap when they were washing up at home or doing laundry at the local creek. Rather than ignore this consumer feedback, the company's management, unaware they'd created a soap that floats, tried to figure out what had happened. After talking to a number of workers at the soap factory, they finally found a worker who had left a machine on by accident over his lunch break, whipping air into his batch of soap. He was initially embarrassed at what he had done, but when told consumers loved the soap, he was eager to show how to make it.

While that story made the rounds of innovation workshops for decades, the reality is even better. The fact is that James N. Gamble, a company chemist and the son of the co-founder, discovered how to make the soap float, tested it and found it to be a benefit to consumers. P&G branded this floating soap, Ivory, and for more than a century it was the leading bar soap in the U.S. One could argue this was the first consumer insight P&G generated. Generating such insights became part of the company's DNA, a legacy that has continued for almost two centuries.

In 1963, P&G decided to get into the coffee business, and they acquired Folger's, a regional San Francisco-based brand that had launched back in 1850. The company saw a chance to acquire a smaller brand with the potential to become a national or even global business. The category leader at the time was Maxwell House, which was founded in 1892 and had grown to control a dominating share of the consumer coffee market. Its slogan, "Good to the Last Drop," was one of the best known taglines among U.S. consumers. General Foods, which owned Maxwell House at the time, would not let a small upstart come in and thrive in this category. Based on its century-old heritage, the company had plans to teach P&G a painful lesson.

For the balance of the 1960s and up until the early 1980s, Folger's remained a distant second to Maxwell House. For years, the Folger's marketing team followed a tested consumer advertising model, basing their claim of a superior product on the fact that the company used "mountain grown coffee—the richest kind." However, P&G decided that if Folger's were to become a business worth investing in, they needed to understand what it would take to get coffee drinkers to make the switch from their current brand. So, they put aside all their assumptions and spent an incredible amount of time and effort to generate new consumer insights about coffee, poring over all the existing category research in addition to an exhaustive amount of custom qualitative and quantitative consumer research.

An interesting consumer insight began to take shape when marketers started to hone in on a simple but powerful question: "What is the gold standard for heavy coffee drinkers?" The "gold standard" was the first cup of coffee you had in the morning. According to their extensive research, consumers paid the closest attention to the aroma and taste of their first cup of coffee in the morning. They counted on it to get them going when they got out of bed. No matter how many more cups of coffee they'd drink the rest of the day, the first cup remained the one they cared about the most.

So, the team set out to make Folger's the consumer's choice for that first cup, figuring the coffee they consumed the rest of the day would follow. P&G worked with its advertising agency to translate this insight into a compelling consumer proposition: "The Best Part of Waking Up Is Folger's In Your Cup." The iconic campaign launched in 1984 and continues to run today.

By the late 1980s, Folger's became the category leader and surpassed Maxwell House in the highly competitive coffee category. And it all started with a hard-working team that knew the importance of generating and leveraging a key consumer insight.

Listening and responding to the voice of the customer

As the P&G Folger's team found, the work needed to truly understand your target audience is hard, expensive and time consuming. Like so much in life, there are no shortcuts to doing it right. The rewards for thoughtfully developing and deploying a combination of qualitative and quantitative research to gain consumer insights will not guarantee success for your communication strategy, but not doing it pretty much guarantees failure.

The mantra of your team should be, "Listen and respond to the voice of the customer." If you follow the techniques outlined in this chapter, you're well on your way to accomplishing this goal.

The Three Most Important Things to Remember about Consumer Research

Dr. Jim Nyce
Independent Consultant, Consumer & Customer Insight, LLC

No. 1

The central premise of the marketing process is that if a company takes the time to truly understand its target consumer, it will be able to design products, programs and messaging that are understandable, relevant and will deliver value to its consumer as well as to the company. Consumer research is the means by which the company acquires the understanding necessary to appropriately tailor its offerings to its consumers, so as to deliver value to them.

Consumer research is conducted to enable consumer learning to guide decisions or strategic business questions facing the company. It is used to identify opportunities and mitigate risks. It may be used to identify consumer attitudes, behaviors, and/or needs that provide opportunities for the company to both deliver value *to* the consumer and derive value *from* the consumer through the development of new products or services. Consumer research is also used to reduce the risks in the implementation of financially significant marketplace initiatives—such as new product introductions, major advertising and/or promotional investments—through pre-testing those initiatives with target consumers prior to launch.

The first and perhaps most critical factor in consumer research is designing the research process with a clear consensus around the **research objective:**

- the business decision or strategy that the research will be designed to inform and guide

- *and* **who** you will be talking to about **what** to inform that decision.

Being clear about **why** you are doing the research guides the identification of **who** you will need to talk to and **what** you will be talking to them about. Clarity and consensus around these three issues are the essential starting points for engaging a research provider—either internal or external to the company—to design and conduct the work for you.

No. 2

Research quality matters a lot! Good judgment is far better than bad research; and, unfortunately, good data and bad data look pretty much the same. Quality flows from careful attention to the quality and representativeness of the research sample, the design of the research tools (questionnaire, discussion guide, etc.), and the compilation and analysis of the consumer data. All of these require the training and experience you will find in skilled marketing/consumer research companies, and choosing a quality research provider is the second critical step in a successful consumer research effort.

No. 3

The *value* of consumer research isn't in the data it generates, but in the impact it has on the decisions and plans it guides. This leads us to the third most important thing to remember about consumer research. While the consumer research process necessarily focuses on the selection of an appropriate target consumer respondent, and the development and implementation of a high-quality research approach, the process is only half complete when the data and results arrive. At that point, the focus must shift to developing the communication materials and processes to ensure that those within the organization who can benefit from the new learning are both informed and inspired to act on it. Unless the results of the work are actually used to guide important decisions and strategies, the entire effort is a waste of corporate financial and human resources.

If consumer research is guided by a clear research objective, conducted by a high-quality research provider, and delivered to the key decision makers within the company in a manner that compels them to incorporate this learning into their decisions, strategies and plans, it can be a powerful source of competitive advantage and growth opportunity identification for the company. ■

Quiz Answers

⬇ Online Exhibit 3.2[1]

Q #1: According to the Census Bureau's American Community Survey, what percentage of U.S. households "speak a language other than English" at home?

Answer: 21.3 % (American Community Survey, 2017)

Q #2: Between 2007 and 2016, the unauthorized immigrant population in the United States:

    a. Increased about 26 %

    b. Increased about 12 %

    c. Decreased about 4 %

    d. Decreased about 13 %

Answer: D, decreased about 13 % (Pew Research Center, November 2018)

Q #3: As of 2017, what percentage of Americans had a passport? (Bonus points: What proportion had one in the late 1980s?)

Answer: 42 % in 2017, compared with 3 % in 1989 (U.S. Department of State, U.S. Census Bureau)

Q #4: What percentage of American households make less than $50,000 per year?

Answer: About 42 % (U.S. Census Bureau, 2017)

Q #5: What percentage of American households are married couples with kids?

Answer: As of 2014, just 16 % of households were married couples with children, down from about 37 % in 1960 (Pew Research Center)

---

1 Links to sources for these quiz answers and to other data, media and examples used throughout the book can be found in the appendix and on our website: www.craftingpersuasion.com

Q #6: In 2014, what percentage of births were to unmarried mothers? (Bonus points: What was the proportion in 1960?)

Answer: Unmarried women accounted for 40% of births in 2014, compared with 5% in 1960 (Pew Research Center)

Q #7: What percentage of Americans have graduated from college with a bachelor's degree?

Answer: As of 2016, one-third of Americans had a bachelor's degree, up from 28% a decade earlier and 4.6% in 1940 (U.S. Census Bureau)

Q #8: What percentage of Asian Americans have graduated from college with a bachelor's degree?

Answer: 55.9% as of 2016 (U.S. Census Bureau)

Q #9: What percentage of American households carry credit card debt?

Answer: About 48% (NerdWallet, 2018)

Q #10: What percentage of Americans by age group say they "often" get their news from a print newspaper (18 to 29 years old; 30 to 49; 50 to 64; and 65-plus)?

Answer: 2% for those 18 to 29; 8% for 30 to 49; 18% for 50 to 64; and 39% for 65-plus. (Pew Research Center, December 2018)

Q #11: What percentage of American adults believe that human beings evolved through natural processes over millions of years without divine intervention?

Answer: As of 2017, 19% of Americans believed in evolution without divine intervention; 38% believed in "theistic evolution" (i.e. evolution but with God guiding the process); and 38% believed God created humans in their present form. (Gallup Poll)

CHAPTER 4

'B' Is for Behavioral Objective

> **"Never confuse motion with action.**
> **Well done is better than well said."**
> —Benjamin Franklin

I f you took a speech class in high school, you likely learned that the primary goal of any speech is to inform, entertain or persuade. When it comes to an overall communications strategy, though, informing and entertaining are nice to have, but the ultimate objective is to *persuade*. This doesn't simply mean changing someone's mind about a particular issue; it means persuading them to take action. This is your behavioral objective, and you need to decide what it is before developing your message.

There's a simple reason for putting this in your communication strategy: The "change in behavior" ultimately delivers the return on investment you want to achieve. Everything you do in communicating with an audience will take resources and time—sometimes a little, and other times an incredible amount. Without that change in behavior, all your effort is in vain. This chapter will explore what factors you should consider when developing your behavioral objective, so you can craft the right messaging strategy for what you hope to achieve.

What should your behavioral objective include?

All behavioral objectives should be SMART—Specific, Measurable, Actionable, Realistic and pegged to a Timeframe). Here's what we mean:

- **Specific**—If you set a goal of convincing young people to buy more product or change a point of view, you're looking too broadly and generally. You'll have a hard time creating a strategy, and an even harder time discerning whether you've succeeded. Alternatively, if your goal is to increase product sales among 18- to 24-year-old men who live in three specific Western European countries by 25% over the next twelve months, that is a specific and measurable objective. You don't always need to be quite that precise, but the closer you can get to the second example rather than the first, the better off you are.

- **Measurable**—As we continue to reinforce: *What gets measured gets done.* The reason measurement can be difficult, particularly with some governmental and NGO challenges, is that the objective is often to decrease a negative, such as "reduce terrorist attacks" or "convert young people away from violent extremism." How will you know if you are winning or losing? What proof allows you to conclude that your communication efforts helped lead to a reduction? Though it can be tricky, you need to define your behavioral objective in some measurable way—not only to know if your efforts worked, but to figure out how you can improve on them the next time.

- **Actionable**—Why bother setting goals that won't make a difference in the long run? While we don't want to set objectives so far in the future they can't reasonably be achieved, we don't want to set ones that are so close in and easy to reach that we haven't made a meaningful impact. The development of a behavioral objective that spells out what should happen next with the target audience needs to be well considered and thoughtful.

- **Realistic**—This is the flip side of "actionable." If you try to eat an elephant in one big bite, you will fail. And if you fail, you might not get enough support to try again. You might lose the support of your management, the enthusiasm of your team, and the energy that all great endeavors need to succeed. Your reach should exceed your grasp, and you should definitely keep your eye on the ultimate prize, but remember to eat the elephant one bite at a time!

- **Timeframe**—Every step in the SMART approach needs to take time into account. It's critical to understand what you can accomplish in the time you have available. Years ago, there was a game show called *Beat the Clock* (which has been imitated, but never matched). The game challenged contestants with physical tests that, on the surface, didn't seem all that difficult. A contestant might be asked to fill a cup with water, using only a tablespoon while balancing a plate on his head. Sounds doable, until the host told the contestant he had only 60 seconds. As you set your behavioral objectives, develop an appropriate timeframe that ensures they are specific, measurable, actionable, and realistic.

Obviously, it's essential your management agrees with your behavioral objective before you begin developing your communication campaign. If you don't have consensus, it could be a very painful (and potentially career-limiting) discussion as to what a "win" looks like. Based on our personal experience in business, nothing is more frustrating than debating what your behavioral objective is *after* the communication campaign begins and the results start coming in. Some will argue your communication campaign was an unbelievable success, while others will just as vehemently claim its complete failure. The only way to keep this from happening is to insist on spelling out your behavioral objective in your ABCDE communication document *before* execution.

Define "the prize"

Put another way, defining your behavioral objective forces you to start out with the end goal clearly in mind. It's a declaration of what you intend to achieve, and it needs to be specific enough that a rational person can evaluate how well the results compare to the original aim. This means you have to do more than just change minds. Yes, it's true you'll have to influence how people think about an issue, *but the job isn't done until you get them to act*. Here are some examples of behavioral action:

- **Political Campaign**—"Vote for John Doe for Congress in November" is your behavioral objective. Your communication campaign is going to include a lot of information on why John is qualified, and you might sway people's attitudes about him, but it won't matter if you don't get out the vote on election day.

- **Brand Launch**—"Download the new cool Simplico app on your phone today" is your behavioral objective. You must generate awareness for this brand launch, but all that effort is for naught if you can't get enough users to download the miracle software that took years to develop and millions of dollars to advertise.

- **Small Business Offering**—"Sign up for our free home delivery" is what you want your customers to do. Since you've invested in the equipment, training and marketing to offer this to your customers, it's essential that you make sure they use it. Full awareness won't matter if enough customers don't actually sign up.

- **Fundraiser**—"We need to raise $100,000 for the neighborhood playground by the end of this year" is what success looks like. As Benjamin Franklin said, "Nothing focuses the mind more than knowing you're going to be hung in the morning." A looming deadline is used all the time (think auctions, PBS fundraisers, etc.) to motivate people. A defined timeframe can spur action and make it easier to measure results.

Of course, even within the SMART approach, you can define your behavioral objectives in all kinds of ways. So, taking a little extra time to set these objectives at the outset of your communication strategy work will pay dividends in the long run. It's the only way that everyone associated with this campaign can know what they're toiling to achieve. And moreover, until you determine the behavior you want you can't possibly know what message you need to deliver. If you want to get an individual to donate $10 to your cause, your message will likely be very different from a request for $1,000.

Keep your time frame in mind

In many cases, you can achieve your behavioral objective in a year or less. Get your candidate elected. Get people to try your new product for the first time. Raise enough money to get the new playground built. These very clear behavioral objectives can be easily measured. But keep in mind that behavioral objectives are often layered, and they might take a long time to achieve. Your ultimate behavioral objective might require one or more intermediate steps, so the communication strategy you are working on right now might amount to one step in a longer process.

For example, in May 1961, when President John F. Kennedy announced that the U.S. would put a man on the moon by the end of the decade, he set a specific, time-bounded and easily measurable goal that integrated a huge sphere of geopolitical considerations at the time. The Soviet Union had shocked the U.S. with its Sputnik launch a few years earlier, and the rising tensions of the Cold War pitted the Russians and American interests not only in science and space, but in any number of cultural and political contests back here on earth. With this speech, Kennedy took that broader context and concentrated it into a goal that was very specific, measurable and actionable. It would be decades before the Berlin Wall came down and the Soviet Union broke apart—and, in many respects, Russia remains a formidable geopolitical adversary to the U.S.—but the specificity and timeframe Kennedy set for the moonshot focused the American and global fight against Soviet communism and provided a clear and tangible first step toward its eventual demise.

Sometimes a behavioral objective might take decades, even several lifetimes, to achieve. Just because it takes a long time to achieve a stated behavioral objective doesn't take away from the value of that effort. In fact, some of the greatest speeches in the world have laid out very aspirational behavioral objectives. And while achieving those visions require tremendous effort and don't happen overnight, those speeches work because their audience knows exactly how the speaker defined what success—or even just the first step toward success—looks like.

That should be your goal as well.

The five-stage marketing funnel process

You might establish a behavioral objective that takes years to accomplish, or it might be modest enough to achieve by next week. Regardless of the time and resources needed, you will want to utilize a proven marketing process that enables you to plan for and, eventually, deliver on those objectives. (See Box 4.1) To do this, marketers use a tried and true process called "the marketing funnel." The funnel advances through five distinct stages:

- **Awareness and understanding**—This is the first phase of achieving your behavioral objective. Is your target audience even aware of the issue you are focused on? Are they aware of your message and position on the subject? What's their current level of understanding (i.e., what do they know that's true and what do they think is accurate but isn't)? They cannot possibly be persuaded if they aren't aware of or don't understand your message.

- **Attitude and consideration**—Once your target audience understands the issue you are focused on, the next step is to shift their attitudes and then work your way into their "consideration set." You need to be on the short list of choices they might be willing to consider. This could be whom to vote for, which movie to see, an alternative to violence, or any one of the thousands of other decisions people make every day. If you are successful in your communication effort, your behavioral objective will make it into the "consideration set" of your target audience.

- **Trial**—This step involves the initial action you want your target audience to take—in other words, the first level of what would qualify as a behavioral objective in action. Depending upon what you are working on, this might be everything you wanted to achieve, such as vote for John Doe on election day. Or your audience might just dip their toes in the water and try your product or make that first small donation. This trial step often involves minimal risk or commitment on the part of the target audience. Think of free samples: If consumers aren't interested in the product, they might toss it in the trash. But if they already started thinking about including the product or brand in their consideration set, they might just give it a try—especially if there's little or no risk. The same goes for non-profits, where an annual contribution to your cause serves as the behavioral objective. If that's asking too much too soon, getting them to attend a fundraising event for the first time could serve as a first step toward that longer-term commitment.

- **Conversion**—This requires a higher, more-committed level of behavior from your target audience. Conversion means they willingly take an action that requires an exchange, where they give something up to get something in return. In the case of products or services, they give up money. In the case of societal causes, they might resolve to stop driving after a few cocktails or decide to donate to a children's charity. And that more-involved behavior then lays the foundation for the ultimate step: a personal referral.

- **Commitment and referral**—This is the highest level of behavior you can ask from your target audience. It goes beyond loyalty to your brand. Not only will they try your product or support your cause, but they will put their own good name and reputation behind it. Generating positive referrals is how new products win in the marketplace, politicians get elected and nonprofits convince the public to support their efforts. Getting to this stage requires hard work, persistence and the efforts of many people. It also requires a well-considered communication strategy that started with the end in mind—a behavioral objective that everyone understood, supported and focused on making a reality.

The Marketing Funnel in Action:
Thomvest Ventures

Like the business titans who star in the television show *Shark Tank*, the partners at Thomvest Ventures provide entrepreneurs the funding and, in many cases, the business expertise they need to scale their fledgling companies. The San Francisco-based venture capital firm has a $300 million fund to invest in startups, mainly in three areas: cybersecurity, financial technologies and sales and marketing innovation.

Thomvest faces a somewhat unusual communications challenge. The Bay Area is home to more than 600 venture capital firms, all competing not just for the next billion-dollar "unicorn" idea but for the wider set of startup investments that produce a solid return, as well. So, building awareness of Thomvest and differentiating themselves from the crowd became a top priority—and the overall goal of the firm's marketing initiatives. It needed to position itself as the preferred venture capital investor for founders and CEOs in industries that fit Thomvest's three areas of expertise. Those founders and CEOs were its target audience, and getting them to select Thomvest as their preferred investment partner is their ongoing behavioral objective.

So, what's the best way to make this happen? Using the Five Stage Marketing Funnel, let's walk through this process:

- **Awareness and Understanding—** In the VC world, you don't need to generate awareness among millions to be successful. You are looking at a much smaller potential audience—more likely in the hundreds. This will consist of company founders and influencers in the three key business categories in which the firm invests. These influencers might include successful entrepreneurs in the space, other VC thought leaders who invest in similar startups, and others who drive the evolution of the industries in which Thomvest invests. Identifying them was the firm's first step toward achieving its behavioral objective.

- **Attitude and Consideration—** Once the firm identified the key influencers in the business sectors in which they sought to invest, it began to generate a greater number of entrepreneurs wanting to work with the firm for their particular companies. When someone wants to start a new business, the first person they tend to seek out is someone else who's already succeeded in the same space. Getting on the short list of VCs that the most promising startup founders would consider was key to achieving Thomvest's behavioral objective.

- **Trial—** When a VC and a startup agree they want to work together, they formalize the financial terms for doing so in something called a "term sheet." This document uses a standard format to lay out the primary terms of financing as well as governance of the startup via board composition and other factors. A hot startup might get more than one term sheet from several VC firms. (In fact, they are hoping they do so they can negotiate the best deal.) Consider this the "trial" phase in the marketing funnel process, since you can't get to a final sale until you generate the term sheet. Thomvest's trial phase focused on efforts to generate discussions with leading entrepreneurs in their fields, culminating in term sheets with multiple promising start-ups.

- **Conversion—** A startup's decision to select a VC's term sheet triggers the creation of the legal documents for the financing itself and culminates in the VC buying shares in the startup. The important things are (a) the start-up gets the funding it needs, and (b) the VC firm gets the opportunity to put its money to work (ideally leading to a very strong return on investment). Getting their term sheets accepted by the CEO of the most promising startups in their fields is how Thomvest measures conversion.

- **Commitment and Referral—** If you want to be a successful VC firm in the long run, it's critical that you have a growing number of CEOs who will give your firm a strong reference to aspiring CEOs of other startups. The best form of marketing is when someone puts their own stamp of approval on what you offer to others like them. Thomvest conducts an annual survey of their portfolio's CEOs to measure how they're doing on referrals. Making sure they have a strong reputation as a great VC firm to work with among this target audience is of critical long-term importance.

In summary, marketing campaigns need to have a well-considered behavioral objective that everyone understands and supports from the outset. The Five-Stage Marketing Funnel can help you think about the various ways you might achieve your objective. It's all easy to outline, but like anything in life, putting it into operation takes a lot of time and resources. Paying close attention to defining your end goal from the start helps focus those efforts, brings everyone on board with the plan, establishes the project's initial parameters and, ultimately, sets the terms by which you'll measure success.

With A (Audience) and B (Behavioral Objective) of the ABCDE Model, we've established the foundation for what we want to say and how we want to say it. Now, with that legwork in place, it's time to turn our attention to what we want the target audience to understand about our message. For that, we look at Content.

Best Advice? Put Emotions and Feelings First

Dr. Victoria Romero
Chief Scientist at Next Century Corporation

Everyone has psychological needs; everyone has certain feelings they crave. Some of us need to feel important—that we're making a difference in the world. Others crave feelings of safety, security, and stability. Others eschew stability; they crave the feeling that they are on the cutting edge of something revolutionary. Some people deeply need to feel attractive. Some deeply need to feel independent.

Many people crave a sense of belongingness—the feeling that they are a part of something bigger than themselves. Some people need to feel respected; others don't care too much about that but deeply care that they feel like the world is fair. The key to understanding how to persuade an audience lies in tailoring your message to fulfill these needs. Note that needs are all about feelings; more often than not, persuasion works through emotions, not facts.

That is not to say that facts are never important. Facts are critical when making decisions about non-emotional topics. (Remember this means topics that are non-emotional *to your audience*). For example, in choosing an investment broker, facts and figures about credentials and past success can be very persuasive. However, as emotions become more involved, the dominance of facts wanes. Even in our investment example, signs of conservative investment approaches will impact people differently depending on their psychological need to feel safe.

As topics become more emotionally charged, facts become ever less important. On highly emotional topics, our emotions drive our decisions. Facts are still involved, but they serve the emotions. We cherry pick the facts that support our emotion-driven positions and dismiss those that don't (whether we know it or not).

Consider the gun debate: there are solid facts on the efficacy of gun control, but these facts don't seem to drive decisions on either side of the argument. Too many people feel too strongly about this issue to avoid making emotional decisions. For example, some people have a very strong need to feel independent. Tying opposition to gun control with affirmation of independence is a powerful, emotion-based argument. Gun control makes many people feel like they are losing part of their independence, while messages opposing gun control support their feelings of independence.

In considering the ideas or products you promote, you must consider how your offering can address your audiences' psychological and emotional needs. Identify these emotions first—then consider how you might use facts to back up these emotions. ■

CHAPTER 5

'C' Is for Conent

> **"Creativity is intelligence having fun."**
> –Albert Einstein

Many companies think of content in terms of their advertising strategy or copy strategy. For our purposes, content refers to a communication strategy, and every communication strategy deals with choices. You will face a great deal of pressure to include every aspect of your organization's program in your communications strategy. You have to fight that. Trying to communicate everything will almost certainly communicate nothing at all. If you overwhelm your audience, they will probably remember nothing—and they are less likely to be persuaded to do anything you want them to do.

A good communication strategy rests on a set of key decisions that collectively define the key conceptual content. What are your options? What are the criteria for the choices you have to make? What is the basis for your decisions? Each part of the communication strategy will have its own choices, and the overall strategy will result in yet another set of choices. After all, the ABCDE Model is not totally linear. It is iterative.

Once we have determined the behavioral objectives, for example, we need to review our audience decisions. In many cases, the behavior we want to change or encourage will require an indirect attack. We might not be able to speak directly to the target audience, needing instead to identify the key influencers through which we can sway the people we intended to reach. So, these influencers become our first target.

What is crucial to remember is that the content decisions you make during this phase are *strategic*. It involves the language of a communication strategy, which defines the "what" of the message—it is what we are trying to communicate. So, this stage is *not* consumer-facing. How you present the message to consumers falls under the delivery stage. When we get to delivery, the "D" stage that comes next, we will work on turning these strategic terms and the entire strategy into something your target audience can relate to and understand.

Trying to develop a program or message or media plan without an established strategy is like hammering boards and laying bricks without a blueprint. You'd never do that, but how often have you either started or been asked to develop an execution without knowing your objective, your strategy or your audience? Spending time at this content stage and putting your strategic thinking in writing delivers remarkable benefits throughout your campaign:

- First, it helps you **clarify your thinking**. Ideas that have been swimming around in your head crystallize when you write them down. One legend of copy strategy development used to say, "Good ideas are invariably strengthened on paper, and weak ideas are exposed for what they are."

- Second, it **provides a vehicle through which you can present ideas** to management and secure their agreement before spending time, resources and energy. Nothing is more debilitating to an organization than finding out after the fact that management didn't agree with the creative premise going in.

- Third, a formal strategy document **ensures everyone involved with the next stage of the model—delivery—is crystal clear on direction**. It keeps the program focused during the creative development phase.

■ Finally, it gives everyone involved **a common basis for the evaluation of the resulting creative execution.** If it is not on strategy, it
deserves no further consideration. End of story.

In the strategic process of developing the content strategy for your communications, you need to re-articulate and refine each of the elements that
got you to this point. So, you will confirm your target *audience* and what
you know about them, and you will declare the *behavioral objective* you are
trying to achieve with your communications. (See Box 5.1) Only when
you have made the key strategic decisions about *who* you are focused on
and *what* you want them to do can you proceed to make your key strategic
decisions about content.

BOX 5.1
Reconfirming Your Behavioral Objective

Once you identify your audience(s) and develop the requisite insights
about them, you need to go back and recheck the behavioral objective of
the target. In the case of influencers, our objective might focus on taking
certain actions that persuade our target audience to change their behavior.
Just think through the steps of your strategy—both short and long term.
What do you want the audience to think and do after receiving your message? This needs to be part of the strategic thinking around content.

Shifts in attitude and thinking are what lead to behavior changes, but changing someone's thinking and attitude are not sufficient goals in and of themselves. In the case of one print campaign from AdoptUSKids, getting people
to recognize they don't have to be perfect to be a great parent was only a
starting point. Ultimately, the nonprofit that connects families with children in
foster care wants to spur people to action—to sign on as a foster or adoptive
parent. (⬇ Online Exhibit 5.1) The Ad Council's iconic drunk driving TV spot
brilliantly overlaid the sounds of a screeching automobile collision on video
imagery of two full beer mugs shattering into each other. The imagery is
stunning, but the straightforward text drove the point home in both the TV
and in the complementary print campaign: "Take the keys. Call a Cab. Take
a Stand. Friends don't let friends drive drunk." (⬇ Online Exhibit 5.2)

It's critical that you clearly articulate the specific action you want your communication to drive. Don't assume it is obvious to your audience.

Content is the core of your communications strategy

All the previous steps that you contemplate and then review as part of your strategic thinking leads to the articulation of the strategic content of your communications. Every step you take after this phase is a function of the strategic content you develop here. This provides the foundation upon which you develop a message that, hopefully, persuades your audience to take action.

In the commercial world, the client will work with its communications agency partners, to develop and agree on this copy strategy. That strategy will then go to teams who specialize in translating strategy direction into impactful words and pictures. Because of this handoff, it is imperative that all the requirements in the strategy are clear and concise. Yet, we know that for many of you, this handoff won't occur. You are not only the owner of the strategy, but the person or persons responsible for the execution, as well.

This might tempt you to think you can skip this step or take a less-disciplined approach to strategy preparation—after all, you know what you want to communicate. Don't do that! The very act of writing this strategy will help you and your colleagues create better programs and messaging. Taking a disciplined approach to content will force decisions and agreements that simply won't happen if you skip this step. And, to craft a disciplined approach to content, you need three critical elements—benefits, reasons to believe (RTB), and tone/character.

We'll do an in-depth exploration of each of these three elements in the next few sections of the book. However, to illustrate how these and other elements of the ABCDE communication model work in real life, we also refer to a number of "online exhibits" here and in subsequent chapters. These examples, each of which illustrates a communication principle, can be viewed on our website: www.craftingpersuasion.com. We invite you to send us examples, both good and bad, so we can include them in future editions of this book. (You can send these examples—URLs, TV ads, print ads, etc.—to info@craftingpersuasion.com.)

Benefits

The benefit is the promise you make to the audience—what they will get in return for adopting the behavior you are trying to spur. What is in it for them if they take the action you desire? Identifying the benefit is akin to answering the audience's main questions: "Why should I care? Why should I do this? Why should I think this way?"

This is easy to understand when you think about the products and services you use every day. (Table 5.1) Sometimes the benefits are obvious. Sometimes they're a little subtler. Regardless, an effective message needs to be based on an accurate understanding of some segment of your audience.

TABLE 5.1 The promise of common products and services	
The Product	**The Promise**
Tide Detergent	Cleaner clothes
Crest Toothpaste	Whiter teeth
Duracell Batteries	Longer-lasting batteries
Coca-Cola	Refreshing soft drink
The Service	**The Promise**
FedEx	Speedy delivery
Allstate	Trustworthy insurance
H&R Block	Maximum tax refund

An example of a direct benefit comes from the U.S. State Department, which posted a Facebook message that encouraged citizens to go to the comments and tag friends planning to travel abroad—providing them a reminder to sign up for the department's Smart Traveler Enrollment Plan (STEP) program. (⬇ Online Exhibit 5.3) Since STEP keeps travelers informed of the latest safety and security updates for U.S. citizens, the direct benefit of this communication was to let the target audience know about a simple way they could show friends and family they care about them.

To be clear, some effective campaigns state the benefits indirectly, yet
the benefits remain clear and grounded in an accurate understanding of
the target audience. In its ad to drum up more blood donors, the American
Red Cross didn't directly state the benefit, yet it's clearly understood. The
"You can make a difference" tagline elicits the positive feeling one gets
from helping someone they might not know. (⬇ **Online Exhibit 5.4**) For the
right audience, that's an extremely powerful motivator.

Benefits can be functional or emotional. Functional benefits can be
very straightforward—faster service, lower calories, better educational
opportunities. Emotional benefits touch a deeper chord—you can save
the life of a child in need, you can change your own destiny, your family
will appreciate you. Emotional benefits require a deeper exploration of
your audience and more substantial insights. And sometimes even the
most polished marketers can get it wrong. Pantene's "Sorry Not Sorry"
campaign centered on the insight that women often felt the need to apolo-
gize when an apology wasn't necessary. (⬇ **Online Exhibit 5.5**) The campaign
speaks to the empowerment of women, which is a terrific story. Yet, the
audience didn't understand the connection between strong women and a
shampoo that promised strong, shiny hair. The play on the word "strong"
didn't work.

Conversely, an extremely effective Dove campaign about the real
beauty underneath all the makeup and Photoshop airbrushing related
directly to the promise the brand was making. The ad begins with a model
wearing no makeup, and proceeds through timelapse video to show the
cosmetic and technological makeover she goes through until her image
appears on a billboard ad for foundation makeup. It's visually arresting,
but it also hammers home with a simple black-and-white frame that reads:
"No wonder our perception of beauty is distorted." It then asks viewers
to sign up for the Dove Real Beauty Workshop for Girls conducted by the
Dove Self-Esteem Fund. (⬇ **Online Exhibit 5.6**)

The Ad Council does outstanding work with both emotional and
functional benefits, often combining those with great effect in their work
for a range of U.S. nonprofits. Similarly, Mothers Against Drunk Driving
doesn't just roll out a wealth of dry statistics to try to change habits and
behaviors. It knows the emotional impact of their message can prove even

more immediate. One of its billboards featured an actual wrecked car against a red background and under the bold white text that read: "Sometimes it takes a family of four to stop a drunk driver." (⬇ **Online Exhibit 5.7**)

Generally, a single-minded focus on one benefit works best, but there are times when we might want to promise more than one. In these cases, when it is absolutely necessary to make two promises, you have some decisions to make. Are these benefits equal in priority, or is one clearly primary and the other secondary? Is one the clear priority, and one just worth mentioning? The classic example is the original Miller Lite advertising: "Tastes Great, Less Filling." Historically, lightness and flavor in a single beer had been considered incompatible benefits, but now, with Miller Lite, you could drink more of a great tasting beer.

As another example, consider the multi-benefit message the U.S. State Department aimed to deliver about its education programs that encourage foreign nationals to study in the United States. The benefits included the quality of education, the future advantages a degree from a U.S. college would confer, and the opportunity to make life better for you and your family when you return home with that education. Depending on the culture, the last benefit might rank as far more important than the more pragmatic, individual benefits.

Whether delivering on single or multiple benefits, they will not have staying power with your audience unless you consistently delivery on that promise. Promises made must be promises kept. That is the secret to building the reputation and value of your program and the messaging that delivers it. So, as part of the content strategy development, you need to declare the benefit the audience will receive if they take the action you desire **and** define a clear path to deliver that very benefit. If you are not certain, you need to think long and hard about your benefit message. If you can't promise that every international student who studies at a U.S. college will get a job when they return home, or that they will get a job and a green card here in the United States, then don't make that promise. Certainly, that is an extreme example, and no one would try that...or would they?

Unfortunately, an organization in Israel promised young Israelis that if they traveled to the United States on a holiday visa, they could remain in the country and get work—which is clearly not legal under U.S. immigration law. Not only were most of these young people caught, but, because they had entered illegally, U.S. immigration law also bars them from ever returning.

Reason to Believe (RTB)

As illustrated in the previous unfortunate example, your target audiences are surrounded by communication that promises too much, exaggerates or just plain lies to them on a regular basis. Because of that, they are understandably going to be skeptical of nearly any promise made to them. You must therefore give them a *reason to believe* (RTB) that you can consistently deliver on the promise you made in your benefit statement. This is the second part of your communication strategy. There are a number of proven methods to reassure your audience of your ability to deliver. Each of them provides meaningful, believable information to help convince your audience.

- **Endorsements**—Is there an authority, a person or an organization trusted by the audience that will recommend you and endorse your promise? For many of the promises organizations make to redirect young people away from violence, the advice and counsel of a trusted friend, family member, or community leader is often effective. Similarly, stated positions endorsed by the National Rifle Association leadership have rallied its supporters behind specific actions, candidates, and decisions.

- **Mechanism of Action**—What about the product makes it work well enough to deliver on its promise? The circular motion and unique bristle design on an electric toothbrush mimics a dentist's cleaning instrument, getting between your teeth and cleaning them better than the up-and-down motion of a traditional toothbrush. The use of a safety belt prevents certain kinds of injuries in traffic accidents. The easier it is for the audience to understand the relationship between the mechanism and the benefit, the better it is for your story. Decades ago, Dentyne suggested that its chewing gum, by rubbing against your teeth and gums, was akin to brushing your teeth. That description made it easier for their customers to visualize how it could deliver on keeping teeth clean and healthy.

- **Product/Service Attributes**—What is it about the way a product or service is organized or put together that can support a given benefit? FedEx has more planes and delivery trucks in more places so it can get your package from A to B faster and more consistently. A safety tire has six steel bands and a unique tread design to ensure safety and hold the road better.

- **Ingredients**—What is it made of and why does that matter? Starbucks touts coffee made with high-quality beans that are sourced in an ethical fashion. The quality of the beans is the ingredient reason to believe (RTB), while the ethical harvesting adds a further dimension.

You have to be careful about how you make these connections. As we noted above, the audience has to see the connection for a given RTB to work. For example, a medical product might advertise that its main ingredient comes from jellyfish, but if there's no explanation of what makes the jellyfish ingredient so important—no description of how it delivers the benefit being promised—then the gambit is ineffective. (⬇ Online Exhibit 5.8) If the product promises to extend your life and it is a well-known fact that jellyfish live for a hundred years, I might be interested in learning more. But let's face it, even that sounds like a bridge too far.

Sometimes you can effectively provide multiple reasons to believe. When Crest toothpaste was introduced, the company promoted its product with endorsement and an ingredient RTB. First, the famous campaign showed a child coming home from the dentist with a "report card" and saying: "Look, Mom, no cavities." (⬇ Online Exhibit 5.9) Second, the brand was the first to include fluoride in its product. Kids had been getting fluoride treatments at the dentist for some time, but this was the first time a toothpaste had offered it for everyday use. And third, the brand got the endorsement of the American Dental Association. Interestingly, the ADA was not a massive, well-known organization, but the name added credibility to the promise of fewer cavities.

These can seem fairly straightforward when it comes to tangible products and services. Providing a reason to believe can be more difficult to discern for public-sector professionals seeking to sway opinion or steer impressionable youth away from terrorism. But even then, researching your target audience and understanding which people and things resonate with them will help you identify RTBs that you can achieve and with which they can connect. The U.S. State Department did an effective job of providing benefits and reasons to believe in Facebook posts from embassies in Afghanistan and Mexico. In Afghanistan, the post underscored American efforts to help battle human trafficking and highlighted ways it can be stopped. (⬇ Online Exhibit 5.10). The embassy in Mexico showed how far women had come in science, technology, and engineering by showing the impressive number of women who worked in these professions at NASA. (⬇ Online Exhibit 5.11)

Tone/Character

Tone is the personality, the attitude, or the look and feel of your message, and it's important because the way you express yourself and your message can have a great impact on how your message is embraced by your target audience. A well-defined tone/character statement represents an additional opportunity to make a connection with your target beyond the science, facts, and functional elements. Importantly, the tone/character of a brand should endure. It's not just about one communication or one program. It is an integral part of the brand's image that should be utilized in any communications and remain consistent over time.

If your brand or message is serious, then you can't be frivolous in your messaging. If your program is intended to touch the hearts of your donors, then every time you engage with them, that tone has to be apparent. That doesn't mean a serious and touching program can't employ some lightness in its execution, but its lightness needs to reflect an element that ultimately touches the heart of the audience. Coca-Cola does this exceptionally well. One of its recent campaigns, called "Taste the Feeling," features everyday interactions with friends that celebrate the good times you have when you are with them. The combination of images, music, and words reminds viewers about similar good times with friends and family in their own lives. (⬇ Online Exhibit 5.12)

A clear tone/character directly affects message development. It guides decisions on wording, casting, style, situations, music, and all kinds of other factors. Within the very same category you can have dramatically different characters or personalities for brands. Where ads for Johnson's baby shampoo might be honest, simple and naturally wholesome—featuring a smiling baby with bubbles on his head—one for L'Oreal can be sexy and sultry with a beautifully coiffed supermodel. (⬇ Online Exhibit 5.13)

Many brands are based on emotional benefits. Beer and liquor are great examples of what are known as "badge brands" because, by consuming them, the consumer makes a statement to the people around them about who they are. Interestingly, research shows that in different situations, consumers will desire different brands. A young executive might order an imported beer with his boss, and he might buy a six-pack of Budweiser for his tailgate with friends. The tone of the messaging to reach the same person in each situation will depend on the brand's desired image. Is it the sophisticated brand for the young executive on the rise, or the friendly and unpretentious brand that you enjoy with your friends? How does your communication look and sound? Is it patriotic and proud, quiet and serious, or heart-wrenching and hopeful?

Sometimes a message can produce effective results through two different approaches to tone/character. Typically, though, one approach will clearly work better than the other. Two public-transportation systems posted communications campaigns that encouraged commuters to remain vigilant about their surroundings. One simply showed an empty end of a New York City subway car with an unattended bag and the text: "If you see something, say something. Be suspicious of anything unattended." (⬇ Online Exhibit 5.14). Another featured the headline, "Do you see anything strange?" beside a photo of an elephant sitting in an empty end of a train car. Under the headline, it said: "Not the elephant, he's going to the circus." And, in an even smaller font, it read: "We're talking about the unattended bag." (⬇ Online Exhibit 5.15)

While the elephant ad tries to tell a serious message in a clever and attention-getting way, the image obscures the story the creators wanted to tell and the action they wanted their audience to take. Admittedly, the image of an elephant on a train has stopping power, but will the audience take the time to read and absorb the entire message?

Fight the urge to use four or five descriptors in your character statement. How would you create a message if you were told it had to be contemporary, simple, optimistic, light and hopeful? How would you integrate confident, social, feminine and contemporary? The odds are, as the executor, you would focus on only a couple of these and pay lip service to the others, or maybe omit them altogether. What if your emphasis wasn't what the strategy owner intended? Three descriptors at the most will get you a better result.

Ultimately, the point is that the tone or character you articulate in your strategy will provide the guidance needed to develop a complete, integrated execution. If you don't articulate the look and feel of the messaging you want, then you can't be upset when the execution comes back with a look and feel you never intended.

Setting the stage for development and execution

Rarely will you have just one program or one communications campaign out in the marketplace by itself. In the case of commercial products, for example, you might have basic, mid-range and premium offerings. It is important for these individual stories to support the positioning and promise of the brand as a whole. If you have a car brand and offer three distinctly different models, you need to understand the audience each is intended to serve, the behavior you desire (presumably a purchase), the insights about that audience and its needs—and, of course, the benefit, reason to believe and tone. All of them need to be understood in the context of the overall brand image and positioning.

You might be too young to remember when Cadillac unveiled a subcompact car, the Cimarron. In this case, the product was part of the problem, but the strategic thinking remains the same. While the Cadillac brand stood for premium, luxury and success—and most of its offerings and marketing supported that promise—the Cimarron signified something else. (⬇ Online Exhibit 5.16) It never took off as the company hoped, and Cadillac shut down the product line within six years.

The same need for brand consistency extends to nonprofits, government departments and NGOs, as well. If you are reaching out to donors to raise money for your charity, whether you provide pure water or fight childhood obesity, you need to know what your audience thinks about your organization and what it stands for. If you have multiple programs in place with simultaneous communications, you need to think of each contact as a piece of the same cloth.

Every interaction with your brand and/or your organization has an impact on your audience, a fact that underscores the need to develop a cohesive and coherent content strategy. Taking the time to create a thoughtful strategy—to develop clear, concise and meaningful choices about the benefits, reasons to believe and tone/character of your message. This will provide the rock-solid foundation you need for the **delivery ("D")** and the **evaluation ("E")** phases of your communication campaign.

Focus on the Key Message

Kimberly Doebereiner
Director, Advertising Development, Procter & Gamble

The most difficult part of any strategy, and the most important, is focus. In almost every case, we want to say more about our product or service than the person we are "talking" to wants to hear. The ability to find the one thing or one thought that is most powerful is a craft worth building. The due diligence to hone a strategy to a single focus is the hardest work your team will do.

The benefit of focus is seen in the creative idea. Think about a great idea you have seen, and you will be able to articulate the focus of the communication. Focus unleashes creativity. Leaving it open for whomever you have developing your content or for your own team may sound like you are "giving them room to explore." In fact, the opposite is true, usually. The greater the focus of the strategy, the better the ideas it helps to generate. ■

CHAPTER 6

'D' Is for Delivery

"Creative without strategy is called art.
Creative with strategy is called advertising."
–Professor Jef I. Richards

Delivery presents us with two significant challenges. One is how we translate our strategy into effective communication campaigns (what we'll refer to as "message"). The other is how we get our messages to connect with our audience (what we'll refer to as "media"). Both need to work or we have no effective communication—and certainly no persuasive communication.

This is an iterative process. Media choices are often decided by the situation on the ground. For example, you might have only a few select options in a given environment. Further, you have a limited budget. So, you might need to determine a medium first. Similarly, media selection can greatly affect messaging. What might work well in a television ad or a YouTube video might not be as effective as a radio spot or a social media campaign. It's fine to circle back and rethink each element as you learn more about your situation.

In this chapter, we will identify the key elements involved in delivering effective communications. We will look at a variety of communication vehicles, from traditional television to YouTube videos and from newsprint to Facebook posts. We will show you how you translate the language of your messaging strategy into words and pictures that can touch consumer audiences.

Delivery: Message

The real magic happens when creative people take the strategy you give them and transform it into understandable, memorable, and persuasive messaging. There are tons of books on how to write creative advertising—some better than others. We will not try to make you a master copywriter, but we will try to give you some basic rules of engagement for telling your story. At a minimum, you will have a greater appreciation for what it takes to create memorable messaging, whether you are evaluating someone else's or developing your own.

Strategy versus execution

Given the amount of time and energy you have invested into the creation of your strategy, part of you will be tempted to simply import those words into your creative execution. While this might get you to a point where your audience understands what you are trying to say, that can only happen if your execution stops them, even for a moment, from thinking about all the other information and data and noise that overwhelms them all the time. Remember, while this strategic message is really important to you, it might not be to them.

How many decisions have you made the first time you saw an ad or another piece of communication? Forget about examples that resemble your program, job, or issue; think instead about important things that are not your primary focus. Perhaps you wanted to buy a new car. It's not a small purchase, so it's an important decision, but it's not something you think about every moment of every day, either. So, how many times do you need to consider the reasons to buy a particular car? How many times does that brand have to reach you and build up its value in your mind? If the automaker's message doesn't stick in your mind, doesn't that reduce the likelihood of it persuading you?

As professionals trying to persuade an audience, our main objective is to translate strategic directives into the words, pictures, sounds, and emotions that will tell our story in a truly memorable way. Before you try to do this with your own program, think about the products, services, and issues that you interact with as a consumer—and then think about communications you have seen that have impacted you the most. Which commercials or articles or videos made you stop and think?

All these memorable messages have some basic elements in common, and we can parse those and learn from them. We will start with two broad topics: what you are *showing* and what you are *saying*. The pictures and the words—no matter the medium or vehicle you use to deliver your message—need to work well together. Even in audio-only formats such as radio, you need to paint a vibrant mental picture with words, so the same concepts apply.

What's the Big Picture?

One thing the following examples all have in common is that a single picture or visual sequence captures the primary message for their audience. [You can find all the following examples on our website: www.craftingpersuasion.com.] The images used in anti-smoking campaigns, for instance, often generate visceral reactions. In one such ad, cigarette butts form what look like rotted teeth in the mouth of a woman whose bright red lipstick and flawless skin suggest she's young and attractive. The dissonance is disturbing on a gut level, and the image delivers the message without needing a word of copy. (⬇ Online Exhibit 6.1)

Apple has developed some iconic ads over the years, including its "Think Different" campaign that associates the brand with great creative minds. (⬇ Online Exhibit 6.2) Many of the folks depicted—for example, Albert Einstein—never used an Apple computer, but the message is that Apple is the choice for you if you want to be like them. Black and white photos of puppeteer Jim Henson and musicians John Lennon and Yoko Ono, accompanied by the "Think different" tagline, convey the idea that Apple products are associated with creative genius.

With product performance claims, the pictures can be pretty straight-forward. Side-by- side comparisons can say it all. Tide used this effectively in one of its laundry detergent ads, which features two photos of the same young man wearing the same white dress shirt. In the photo on the left, the shirt is smeared with food; in the image on the right (after it was cleaned with Tide) the shirt is pure white. (⬇ Online Exhibit 6.3)

One caution, though: Don't spend so much time dramatizing the problem that you fail to showcase how your offering solves it. Too often the humor and the drama stem from the problem itself, but it can be tempting to overstate it for dramatic effect and, thus, overshadow the solution. Making sure you deliver an effective "Big Picture" requires that you satisfy four basic requirements:

Be about the brand: Make sure the picture you've chosen to tell your story is quickly and easily associated with your brand and message. Don't ask your audience to stretch too far to get the point you're trying to make. For example, consider a pair of Land Rover ads—one that shows a bear looking up from a lofty alpine outcropping, another that shows a mountain goat perched atop a Land Rover that's on a lofty alpine outcropping. (⬇ Online Exhibit 6.4) They both suggest Land Rovers can go anywhere, and they both reflect a great selling point for thrill seekers. But the latter image gets to the point better than the other.

Be recognizable: The audience needs to know, as quickly as possible, who is talking to them. Don't be afraid to show your brand name and/or logo early and often. The story can't really be told without the brand. In fact, if it can be told without the brand, you have a bigger problem because it means the story is generic. In television commercials, this brand reveal ideally happens in the first five seconds. With the internet and channels like Facebook and Snapchat, it *has to* happen within the first three seconds, because consumers can immediately skip content on these platforms. Visuals and other assets can be very effective at delivering this factor.

Two other Land Rover video spots provide a good contrast on the importance of clearly identifying your brand. The first ad, for its Range Rover Sport, features the vehicle flying through the Arabian Desert. (⬇ Online Exhibit 6.5) It's beautiful, with slow motion shots interspersed with views of the SUV speeding across the dunes, sand billowing in its wake. However, you don't see the name of the model or the Land Rover logo until the very end of the 30-second commercial.

The automaker's "Dragon Challenge" commercial for the same SUV is equally arresting. But rather than rely solely on the breathtaking views of the Range Rover Sport driving around 99 curves and up 999 stairs to reach the top of misty Tiananmen Mountain in China, the ad includes a text introduction within the first few seconds: "Land Rover Presents the Dragon Challenge." (⬇ Online Exhibit 6.6) Immediately within its 30-second runtime, you know the brand being advertised. Both ads have plenty of drama and storytelling, and both feature stunning video, but the brand is instantly recognizable only in the second ad.

Be simple: On social media and mobile devices, the constraints of the media are obvious. You have little time and space to accomplish your goal. However, the idea that you have more time and space in a television commercial or print ad is an illusion. You don't. To get your audience's attention, you are competing with hundreds of other things every time they interact with your message. Keep the big picture simple. Clorox came up with a great example that's brilliant in its simplicity. The image shows seven happy boys, sitting and facing the camera with their stockinged feet splayed out toward the viewer. (⬇ Online Exhibit 6.7) All the boys' socks are snowy white save those of one, which are gray. The caption, "Guess who forgot the Clorox," says it all.

Grab your audience's attention. Think about what stops you when you are watching television, looking at a video, or scrolling through your Facebook posts. Almost invariably, it's the visual—that arresting picture or scene. Whether a Harley-Davidson print ad that features a motorcyclist driving through a stunning big sky landscape, or a tight shot of the back of a bright red Corvette, (⬇ Online Exhibit 6.8 and 6.9) three things can make your visuals stand out:

1. **Clean and simple**—Don't try to put everything in the picture. Closeups are often very effective when using people as your visual.

2. **Bold, contrasting colors**—Your choices will depend on the tone and character of your strategy.

3. Motion—The human eye will be attracted to movement versus a still picture.

Of course, you need to keep plenty of other factors in mind when considering what visual will attract attention. For example, steer clear of "borrowed interest," like showing an attractive person or a bold new concept car when they have nothing to do with your message. Remember that grabbing the audience's attention is only a starting point. If the visual isn't on brand and recognizable, the odds of delivering persuasive communication decline dramatically.

What's the Big Idea?

Along with the Big Picture, great communication has a "Big Idea"—those words that tell the story in an arresting, memorable, and persuasive way. It's often the brand slogan or a memorable quote from a brand's advertising. Just like the process used to develop the Big Picture, developing the Big Idea requires that you use copy that is on brand, recognizable, simple, and attention-grabbing. People still remember some big ideas long after a brand has stopped using the words in their advertising.

FIGURE 6.1 **Examples of iconic "Big Ideas"**		
The Brand	**The Big Idea**	**Launch Date**
Nike	Just do it	1988
Miller Lite	Tastes great, less filling	1974
McDonald's	You deserve a break today	1971
Avis	We try harder	1963
Clairol	Does she or doesn't she?	1957

Do you recall the company that promises you that "You're in good hands" (Allstate), or the one that guarantees delivery "When it absolutely, positively has to be there overnight?" (FedEx)? These are not just strategy words. They are promises that grow out of the strategy, for sure, but they are insightful and memorable, as well.

Nike understood that the biggest challenge to physical activity was inertia; there were always reasons to put exercise off (hence: "Just Do It"). Miller knew that its target consumers were not looking for diet beer with fewer carbs and calories; they wanted a beer that allowed them to drink more without feeling bloated (hence: "Tastes great, less filling"). McDonald's was trying to give moms an excuse to make its burgers and fries a regular part of the family routine (hence: "You deserve a break today").

Avis was a distant second to Hertz in the car rental business. So, the company owned up to this position as a point of pride, embracing its role as an underdog because, well, they have to try harder to compete (hence: "We try harder"). Clairol had two challenges. First, women didn't want to admit they colored their hair. They wanted the world to think their hair was naturally beautiful. Second, home versions of hair color products were not very good at the time, and friends and family could tell when a woman had used them. Clairol's promise was that people couldn't tell if your hair was natural after using it (hence: "Does she, or doesn't she?"). They could have just said that Clairol was so close to natural color that no one could tell, but doesn't their Big Idea—which people still remember decades later—say it better?

Whatever the topic and however you state it, the Big Idea must still reflect the key elements of your content strategy. It absolutely must capture the benefit, and it needs to reflect the tone and character of your strategy, as well. The reason(s) to believe can appear in other parts of the communication, but it and every other aspect of the communication—style, color, music, actors, etc.—need to support the content strategy as captured in that Big Idea.

Horses for Courses

Our UK friends use the phrase, "horses for courses," to explain the importance of choosing the right tool for the situation you face—the right horse for a given set of racetrack conditions. In this case, we use the same idea to stress the importance of understanding where your audience will likely engage with your message and how they will interact with it. Take radio, for example, where you have no choice but to give up the power of images and rely on the power of words, instead. This is a lost art for many creatives, but it can be extremely powerful when done well.

Ogilvy UK developed a brilliant example of the power of words for Dove's Self-Esteem Project for girls. (⬇ **Online Exhibit 6.10**) The radio spot started with a welcoming voicing saying: "The more someone makes you think about your body, the harder it becomes to ignore. Your tongue, for example. Usually, you hardly notice it's there. But when I mention it, you can feel your tongue bumping against your lower front teeth, the tip just resting on them." From there, the script describes what most of us would only notice about our tongues if we were prompted to do so (as the ad does). "A few seconds ago, you hardly noticed your tongue, but just one message ensured you can't stop thinking about it," the script says before introducing the Dove Self-Esteem project. "Now, imagine the hundreds of messages girls are exposed to every day, subtly changing the way they think about their bodies." Similar spots for breathing and blinking were equally memorable.

Of course, a thoughtful combination of words and images can be as or more powerful. However, if you have the need and the budget to deliver your message on television, remember it has limits—as all media do. An online video has some of the same strengths and weaknesses as television, but with the unique benefit that the viewer can replay multiple times and then send it to a friend, potentially giving you a built-in endorsement.

Consider also the device your audience will likely use to view or hear your message. A television screen or computer monitor provides one set of parameters for your videos. But if your audience is primarily going to see your message on a smartphone, then you need to think about the size of the picture, the quality of the sound, and the length of the message.

Since many organizations don't have significant marketing and advertising budgets, let's take a look at some of the most cost-efficient tools available today. What you will find, however, is that most of the factors we discuss apply across the media spectrum.

Instant recognition

With Facebook, all you have is three seconds to engage your audience. After that, you can safely assume your audience will move on to the next post or click through to something else. So, it helps to think about the other medium that must convey a story in such a compressed period—billboards. As you drive down the highway, your eyes are (hopefully) focused on the road, your mirrors, and the traffic around you. Some portion of your attention will be diverted to the music on your radio, the conversation with the person next to you, or the kids roughhousing in the back seat.

Yet, even with all this happening, odds are good you've still noticed a high-impact billboard like the clever one sponsored by the Colorado State Patrol. (⬇ Online Exhibit 6.11). The CSP billboard features a red car crumpled into the back of a blue semi-truck trailer, with the tagline, "Tailgating isn't worth it." The billboard material itself appears crumpled at the point of impact to heighten the drama. Hard to miss that message, even zooming down the highway at 65 miles per hour. Making a similar, quick-but-memorable impact will help get your message across on Facebook, as well.

The mobile experience

Most of your audience will experience Facebook, YouTube and other social media on smartphones, so you need to design your message for a smartphone screen. It's a small canvas. Eye tracking tells us users first look at pictures, so this is where you want to put your most important information, not in the caption. Think of the audience as driving by this "billboard," and keep the visual and the copy simple and legible. After processing the pictures, users look at the captions and then, finally, look at the "handle"—the icon that shows who the message is from and typically delivers the brand signoff.

As you think about your design for an immediate image impact, also remember to take full advantage of the size of the screen. When sizing your videos or graphics, pay attention to the platform requirements. Will viewers be looking at the screen in a portrait or landscape position? Will your site adjust to their screen positioning? If you have to shoot the video or visual two ways, anticipate that in advance of your production session. Having to go back and set it up again can get expensive.

Design for no sound

While many of the members of your audience will have access to sound, make sure you convey your story without it, as well. In many situations, they will be viewing your message with the sound off, with it turned too soft to hear, or in loud environments. A technique the authors have used for years to evaluate television commercials is to mute the sound and see if we can still understand the story. Sound is a bonus, but don't depend on it to deliver your essential message.

Evaluating the "Big Picture"—Facebook examples

While we continue to learn more about the most effective use of tools such as Facebook, the factors we already discussed appear to be very useful in generating engagement. Let's look at a few Facebook posts from a variety of organizations to see how each of the four main drivers of effective execution play out on the platform:

Keep it on brand: Many of the U.S. Embassies around the world post outreach and engagement initiatives on their Facebook pages. Some of these posts work better than others. The Embassy in Pakistan put up an excellent video that sought to teach Pakistanis about the lives and perspectives of Muslims in the United States, aiming to highlight both the diversity of American Muslims and their common bonds as U.S. citizens. (⬇ Online Exhibit 6.12) The embassy's post said simply: "Who are American Muslims? Watch this video—you may be surprised by what you learn!" Then, the video itself featured famous athletes (e.g. Muhammad Ali), U.S. Representatives, artists and a variety of other individuals of Islamic faith. The point of "keeping it on brand" is to remain consistent with the overall brand message, and this video does an excellent job of reinforcing the message that America is inclusive and multicultural.

Make it recognizable: A strong, prominent brand image from the very start of the communication is critical to engagement. We recommend that you don't depend on text alone to deliver your branding. Rather, right from the outset of your message, ensure that you make full use of your brand's executional elements—logos, colors, fonts—as well as the assets of a given program and campaign (e.g. music and visuals).

Antonia Saint NY, a fashion footwear line, did this quite well in a two-part communication plan it ran on Facebook. (⬇ Online Exhibit 6.13) By posting the name of the brand immediately and letting visuals carry the story, the video instantly let's viewers know who's talking to them—despite using no voiceover whatsoever. Meanwhile, in initial versions of the outreach, the Facebook page prominently featured a Kickstarter logo at the time, clearly asking for funding from visitors sold on the concept.

Save the Children likewise made its brand clearly and immediately visible in its Facebook post soliciting donations to feed hungry children in East Africa. (⬇ Online Exhibit 6.14) Prominently displaying the brand from the outside, combined with the use of a consistent look and feel over time, can help increase the audience's rapid recognition of your Facebook communications.

Keep it simple: The U.S. Embassy in the Philippines posted a simple but effective video for its social media campaign, "#FriendsPartnersAllies." (⬇ Online Exhibit 6.15) Using only the three words in the hashtag, a series of still photos and some background music, the embassy staff managed to illustrate the strength and the mutual benefit of the alliance between the two countries. Even stripped of the text, the images embodied the cooperative spirit the U.S. Embassy sought to underscore with its campaign. Using just those three words in the video helped build a foundation on which it could build subsequent messages as part of its communication strategy.

Grab their attention: Promo.com pulled off a clever little video to draw Facebook users' attention to ads for its easy-to-use promotion video production service. (⬇ Online Exhibit 6.16) The short, 10-second video features a young boy on a running track, wearing 1980s sweatbands and workout gear, dancing away to a jam that pumps from an old boom box. It's cute, funny and catchy, but it doesn't distract from the simple text that runs across it: "Running a small business? Give it a big marketing boost. Promo. Make your own marketing videos." The image, the movement, the brevity and the clear messaging in the ad combine to grab viewers attention.

YouTube—Four Drivers of Effective Executions

YouTube shares the same drivers as Facebook communications—keep it on brand, make it recognizable, and grab their attention—but it adds one key element to the mix that can make good executions especially effective: making it connect.

Make it connect: When they're done well, videos on YouTube can deliver a deeper level of engagement with your audience. YouTube and Google are the world's largest search engines. Success with YouTube videos stems from uploading great, search-optimized content that *your audience can find and view, want to see again and again, and want to share with others.* That combination kicks off a virtuous cycle—the more your video is searched, the more metatags it gets, the more it pops up in search, and the more it gets seen. And the more good videos you post, the more you fuel this cycle.

Keep it on brand: As with the Facebook examples above, you want to be sure your message clearly connects to your benefit and brand image. You need to provide the audience a reason to watch and a reason to engage with your communication. That might mean entertaining them, informing them, or identifying with them, but it must bridge between your brand to their needs and interests.

Make it recognizable: With videos, clear branding at the beginning *and throughout* the message is key. Don't depend on a short logo pop-up at the end of the video, because the audience might not still be watching. As we noted earlier, a consistent look and feel—for example, a signature opening to each of your videos—can help drive recognition. A great example is a Dior spot that features actress Natalie Portman. (⬇ **Online Exhibit 6.17**) From the brand name in the opening shot to the logo bug in the corner throughout the ad, the brand's name—not to mention its sultry character—comes across during every second of the video, leaving no doubt about who's behind the ad.

A Mr. Clean video accomplishes the same brand recognition with a different approach—by featuring its iconic Mr. Clean character. As a woman frowns in discouragement at a food spill on her kitchen stove, a buff animated Mr. Clean swoops in to rescue her, only to be revealed at the end of the ad as her schlubby husband, winning her heart by cleaning the house. The Mr. Clean character is so deeply associated with the brand, its appearance just seconds into the ad makes clear who it's from and what it's for. (⬇ **Online Exhibit 6.18**)

Grab their attention: Viewers are probably doing something else when they see your message execution. They may be scrolling through their news feed or searching for a particular video. The first job of your communication is to stop them in their tracks. And grabbing attention needs to be about what's in it for them, and the helpful information or the enjoyment they will get out of it. It needs to give the viewer a reason to watch. Telling a story and/or inspiring your audience are two proven ways to grab the attention of your target audience, and it's worth thinking a bit more about them here.

■ *Tell a Story*—Video can tell a story well, and some of the most-effective stories have a surprise twist. In a wonderful video spot from the Ad Council's "Love Has No Labels" campaign, various sets of romantic partners, friends, or families interact behind a screen that digitizes them into pixelated skeletons. (⬇ Online Exhibit 6.19) After a few brief moments—perhaps a kiss, an embrace, or a brief dance—they step out from behind the screen in a series of big reveals that underscore the many configurations that love can take—in terms of race, sexual orientation, disability, religion, and so on. The video flies in the face of most of our recommendations about early recognition and being on brand, but it does such a great job of telling a story that it keeps viewers engaged long enough to reveal the answers.

■ *Inspire your Audience*—Some brands take a position, engaging in what is now called "purpose marketing," in which they associate themselves with a higher benefit. The Always brand is a great example. In many parts of the world, a lack of feminine hygiene products limits girls' lives. During their periods, they remain at home, missing out on school and other formative life experiences. The Always brand started their purpose marketing with a very open business benefit by introducing girls to Always products for free and, thus, building brand loyalty for the future. But it also decided to become a brand that stood up for girls. In a powerful video, Always featured interviews with girls and young women, who discussed the limits society and culture places on them. (⬇ Online Exhibit 6.20) They wrote the limits on large white boxes. As the tone of the commercial changes and it introduces the "Unstoppable" theme, the girls start wrecking the boxes, standing on them, or destroying walls made of them—a symbol of defiance against those limits. The "Like a Girl" campaign is about far more than feminine hygiene.

A note on traditional television and print

Not surprisingly, the factors we have discussed for YouTube videos can be directly translated to traditional television executions. Often television executions get extended life as YouTube videos, as long as the audience can find them—hence the value of connectivity.

Similarly, print executions have many of the characteristics of Facebook presentations. While consumers may be more involved in television/video spots, they often page through print and social media content as they're doing other things. Arresting the attention of your target audience remains the key challenge.

Evaluating creative messages

In the commercial environment, the client creates their copy and communications strategy, often with considerable help from their agency. But then they give that strategy over to a creative team to turn into an arresting, understandable, memorable, and persuasive message. Most of our students at the USMCC did not have the luxury of an agency. They often were the people who handled both the strategy and the execution.

But whether you have a large budget and an agency or run solo and on a shoestring, you need to ask the same question once you have a creative execution before you: *Is it on strategy?* If it's not, send it back and start again. It's always possible you defined the wrong strategy at the outset, but if you fully believe in your strategy, then nothing should sway you from staying on it. You might love the execution. The recommended spokesperson might excite you. You might love the big picture and the big idea. But if the message is not on strategy, it probably will not go anywhere with your target audience.

During the 2019 Super Bowl, for example, Burger King took a huge risk by featuring footage of Andy Warhol eating a Whopper for 45 seconds. This $7.5 million investment resulted in the weakest performance since 2010 on every metric tracked by the Ace Metrix qualitative scores. It was also the lowest-scoring ad in the USA Today Ad Meter, in 58th place. The company's CMO said the rankings did not concern him; he focused instead on an increase in perception. That last place finish resulted in more than 4 billion impressions, so was this an example of an ad that was "so bad it was good?" Did Burger King get lucky, or just swing and miss in front of a massive crowd? It's an interesting point to contemplate.

Your ability to evaluate messages will become increasingly thorough as you internalize the ABCDE process. Until then—and even every so often afterward—we suggest you stop and force yourself to fill out this communications evaluation grid (Figure 6.2) to ensure you're staying on strategy.

FIGURE 6.2
The communications evaluation grid

Questions	Answers
What is the **audience** that this communication is aimed at, and is it the one in your strategy?	
What is the **audience insight** that is the basis for this communication, and is it the one in your strategy?	
What is the **behavioral objective** that is the focus of this communication, and is it the one in your strategy?	
Regarding the content:	
• Does the communication speak to the benefit you have declared?	
• Does the communication focus on the reasons to believe you have identified?	
• Is the tone/character of the communication consistent with your declared tone and character?	

Once you answer these questions and feel confident the message aligns with your strategy, you can assess the creative delivery. Again, consider a few basic questions as you go through this process (and note that these reflect the key drivers of effective communication on Facebook, YouTube, and almost any other medium you choose):

- **Is it "On Brand?"** Does the execution—the words and pictures—fit with the nature of your brand and this particular copy strategy?

- **Is it Recognizable?** Is the brand identified early and often?

- **Is it Simple?** Is there a big picture and big idea that clearly tell your story?

- **Will it Grab the Attention of your Audience?** Why do you believe that?

To help you develop your own strategy work, we put the communications evaluation grid and an overall strategic framework on our website, www.craftingpersuasion.com. We encourage you to print it out and use it as a tool to help develop your communication strategy. (We also use the same strategy grid to evaluate the case studies included in Chapters 12 and 13.)

Delivery: Media

With the audience identified, the strategy confirmed, and the possibilities for creative delivery properly assessed, the next step is to consider the available vehicles for reaching each audience. Some of these decisions will be a function of simple realities. Media availability differs from one market to the next. In some countries, mobile phones are the only mass media readily available, while radio still dominates in other markets. Your budget might dictate your options—both for production of the execution and for purchasing the media. A small budget might push you toward a less expensive production on social media; a much larger purse could bring in higher production values and big television ad buys. If done well, both can be equally effective.

You need to first ask yourself about your audience's media habits. Just because television is available and you have the budget to use it doesn't mean your audience will find your messages there. Television might not be where your audience is looking. As with the basic audience questions outlined in Chapter 3, don't assume you know the answers. Do some homework on the media usage of your target audience.

Similarly, take time to consider a variety of vehicles and find the best to tell your story. Different media have different strengths. Visual media like television and video provide the ability to tell a story that, with good execution, can deeply engage an audience. And while radio often is considered a reminder medium in many countries—used to reinforce a message delivered mainly through another vehicle—it remains the primary vehicle in many places and situations.

And, again, remember that this entire ABCDE process is iterative. You might start with one audience, but as you gain further insight, you might decide to shift the audience. You might start with a benefit but find that you can't support it with reasons to believe, so you reconsider and adjust. In the case of your creative execution, you might have developed a great television spot or print ad, only to realize that these might be the wrong media to reach your targets—or, worse, realize you just don't have the funds to run a meaningful level of support.

So, you circle back and determine how your execution needs to be revised for the media you have available. With a little patience, a good media model, and the discipline to follow through, you can always find a way!

How to Get Great Work From Your Creatives

Elena Gold
Chief Commercial Officer of Before Brands

Your ability to inspire the agencies and people who work for you can yield either a business-building advertisement or become a total waste of your marketing resources. I've worked with a wide variety of outstanding agencies over the past 20 years, and the most important lesson I learned is this: The marketers are at fault when they do not get the best work out of their agencies.

I can say this because I have made many, many mistakes. We do not always provide the right information because we have not done the right research, or the briefs we provide have too much noise and are not succinct or inspirational. Yet, we expect "award winning creative." There is plenty of information in this book about how to do the up-front strategic work right. Assuming the brief is strong, I have followed three core principles over the years which significantly increase the odds of getting great work from the folks on whom you rely to create powerful and impactful advertising and marketing messages:

Give your agency partners enough time. *Your lack of planning is not their emergency.* It takes as long as six to nine months to get impactful creative, depending on the brand and category you're working on. There should be enough time for exploration, getting feedback from consumers, and reiteration. If you rush this, then, the output will be "rushed" and not as effective. Agencies are very thoughtful about how much time they need to get it right. If you want to do something quicker, ask them at what expense the time savings will come.

When working with your agency, remember what your mother always taught you in dealing with people: _Be nice._ The people who work on your marketing campaign do not want to disappoint you. Quite the contrary; they typically have worked very hard on your business and are very proud to show-case their work. It is a false assumption to believe agencies have thick skins. In fact, creatives usually have *very* thin skin. If you have ever tried to come up with anything creative, you will understand why. So, be truly and genuinely respectful when you hear their ideas for the first time and provide feedback. Remember the human factor in all of this. Treat everyone how you want them to treat you, no matter how much stress you might all be under. Keep in mind that sometimes the first round of creative is just that—a first round. It usually takes a collaborative effort to make things better. With the right feedback and encouragement, I've seen marginal first round creative turn into truly outstanding work by the time it was finished.

Know when and how to walk away. Creative teams do sometimes get tapped out on a business or brand assignment. If the agency is not delivering after multiple rounds, the creative brief is sound, and you've worked hard to inspire your agency partners, then sometimes it is time to ask for a different creative director and/or creative team. I would not recommend switching ad agencies just because one campaign is not working out. In the end, every agency has the same conundrum: they have some folks who are very talented and some who are not. You have the right to and should ask for their best team. But if things are not working out, you typically can get a lot more done by working with your existing agency rather than taking the time and effort to have a totally new agency get to know you and your business. And if your existing agency knows their account is "on the line," they will work incredibly hard to prove you made the right choice in deciding to stay with them.

Working with advertising agencies and creatives can be very frustrating at times. But it can also be some of the most rewarding work you do in your career—if you do what great clients do. *Provide the right strategic framework. Follow the principles outlined above. And then let them do what they do best.* You hire an agency to produce outstanding creative that builds your business or champions your cause. Clients almost always get the creative they deserve—so make sure you do your part to enable them to do their very best work for you. ■

CHAPTER 7

'E' Is for Evaluation

> **"What gets measured gets managed."**
> –Peter Drucker

I f you can't measure it, you probably shouldn't do it—whether a communication campaign, a promotional program or a specific event. Too often, we hear that a leader agrees with the idea of measurement, but then develops a communication program that doesn't really lend itself to any easy measurement. They dismiss those concerns by saying they'll measure it "the next time"—the ultimate form of metrics procrastination. It's much more efficient and effective to dive in and figure out the metrics by which you identify progress or a lack of it in the very beginning, so you can build the most impactful programs. Besides, we've found over the years that adages attributed to Peter Drucker are right 100 % of the time. So, make sure everyone on your team agrees on the importance of clearly defining your behavioral objective before any execution begins.

Before you undertake virtually any communications effort, you need to determine how to measure it, and then make sure your management agrees with that measurement. Over decades of collective practices, we've observed all too much action taken for action's sake alone. That approach burns up resources and burns out people with little, if anything, to show for it. In fact, we'd like to add a corollary to the Drucker quote: "What gets measured gets managed *and what gets rewarded gets done.*" The people deciding on those rewards want to see evidence of success, so it's critical to agree on the definition of success upon which the rewards will be based.

Most of that evidence will emerge through an ongoing evaluation throughout the "five-stage marketing funnel," which we discussed in Chapter 4. Any effective communications initiative relies on its ability to move your target audience through the five steps in that funnel, and at each of those stages, there are metrics and tools that help measure progress—and, thus, measure the success of your program as it develops. This is critical, because generally the five-stage progression is linear: *awareness and understanding* lead to *attitude and consideration*, which lead to *trial*, which leads to *conversion*, which leads to *commitment and referral*—and ultimately moves people to the point at which they change their behavior. A clear and objective measurement of the audience's progression through the funnel illustrates how each stage builds on the others and reveals ways you can bolster your communications.

Evaluation throughout the five-stage marketing funnel

As a starting point, we need to know whether our communications have moved the audience into the big end of the funnel. Have we reached our target audience and, if so, have we reached them with enough frequency to break through the surrounding noise? Rarely does a single exposure get people through the funnel and to our ultimate goal of behavioral change. Each medium will have a method to measure both *reach* and *frequency*. Reach covers the number of people who see and/or hear the message. Frequency involves the number of times they see/hear the message in a given time period. If your media selections don't have sufficient reach or frequency to move the audience into and through the funnel, you need to reconsider the media you are using.

Media options change and evolve, of course, and increasingly the audience self-selects what they see and how often they see it. The world of media metrics has changed dramatically in recent years, and it will continue to do so, but measuring initial success still goes back to reach and frequency. With that in place, we can start to evaluate progress through the funnel:

- **Awareness and understanding:** Exposing an audience to a message does not guarantee they'll connect with it. So, you need a way to measure connection (i.e., awareness and understanding). If your media plan appears to be reaching your audience with sufficient frequency, yet they remain unaware of your message, you might have a problem with creative execution. You might make an ad or communication available on a medium that provides you detailed reach and frequency information, but that doesn't necessarily mean your audience has seen or heard it. Is it breaking through the clutter? Is it memorable? Is it on brand and recognizable? Then, once you know the audience is aware of your message, you need to evaluate whether they understand it. Do they perceive your message as the promise of a benefit for them? Are they buying your reason to believe? If they are aware but don't understand your message, again, you need to review your execution. Is it simple? Is it clear? Is it properly targeted to your audience?

- **Attitude and consideration:** Changes in attitudes rarely occur in a flash. Attitudes evolve over time, often slowly and sometimes imperceptibly. A communications program often needs to convert the audience to at least a "neutral" attitude before the message earns any consideration. Then, it typically takes a bit more evolution to get the audience to the *trial* stage and initial action that follows. These attitude changes demand a deeper understanding of your target audience and insights into what makes them tick. These insights will have led to your communications strategy and execution, but they also need to be continuously tracked to see if you are moving the needle—and what factors seem to be most effective at accomplishing that.

- **Trial:** The trial phase begins when your communications have tipped the audience past the consideration and to the point at which they are willing to take a chance on your offering. The likelihood of trial depends greatly on the risk and the potential reward involved in the trial. This opens a variety of evaluation and measurement possibilities to identify an approach that fosters greater engagement—from tracking the use of coupons to running A/B tests, which use direct comparisons of two executions to determine their relative effectiveness. In the case of countering violent extremism, this trial phase would involve a young person's first willingness to take a step away from violence and toward a more positive action. Generating that trial might come from something as simple as getting those individuals to engage in a positive civic program or attend an event sponsored by a group with an alternative position. Trial isn't a one-off step, and you might need to go through a variety of trials to promote greater conversion. Measuring the success of each initiative will show which programs are getting people to convert, and which programs are dying on the vine.

- **Conversion:** Successful communications lead the audience to our desired behavior. Conversion is a key step because, by converting, the audience has broken through the inertia of negative behavior or inaction. As such, measuring conversion rates can provide guidance for both sides of that key tipping point—another gauge for the success of your trials, but also an early indicator of how much momentum is building toward *commitment and referral.*

- **Commitment and referral:** The ultimate goal is to have the conversion not only become permanent, but to go beyond loyalty all the way to commitment. Ideally, the people who commit to your product, service, cause, or desired behavior become advocates for it, as well. They become references on your behalf. They're typically viewed as less biased influencers. And if there's a setback with your product or cause, they're more likely to continue to support and perhaps even defend you. It's critical that you understand not only how large a committed audience you're developing, but also the depth of their commitment. That depth might be hard to measure without a shock to the system, but understanding it ensures you maintain a cooperative partnership and do not breach trust.

Classic evaluation tools

The good news is we can measure each stage in the communications funnel. While some phases of that journey might be much harder to evaluate than others, the various consumer measurement tools we discussed in Chapter 2 can provide the insights you need. In fact, these tools have been used for generations to successfully measure performance, and we're just getting better at knowing where and how to deploy them. Media metrics. Habits and Practices. Usage and Attitude. Tracking studies. You use them to measure your audience's position on your *behavioral objectives* prior to your communications efforts (pre-study) and then *evaluate* progress afterward (post-study).

We recognize that for many of the communications challenges you face, the time and money it will take to change behaviors can be substantial. Therein lies the value of having a consistent, long-term strategy that can build over time and gradually move the audience, as well as a comprehensive plan for evaluating it. Communications strategies and programs that change with the winds will do little to shift ingrained attitudes and beliefs, and will do even less to change resulting behaviors.

To be sure, it's often difficult to find a meaningful measure for a particular behavioral change. This is especially true when the desired behavior is the lack of an action (e.g., reducing the number of terrorist attacks). The number of factors that impact the desired behavior, which can go well beyond your communications efforts alone, can dramatically complicate your ability to evaluate effectiveness. But you need to be able to determine whether you've made an impact. Is there a surrogate behavior that we can measure to give us perspective? What's the amount of change being observed? Is it going in the right direction? How much did it cost you in resources to achieve that level of change—and was that investment justified?

In the end, it boils down to the return on your investment. Your investment of money, certainly, but also your investment of other resources, such as time, staff, and goodwill. As with almost anything in business or in your environment, resources are a zero-sum game—even if it seems like some programs manage to get unlimited funding while yours starves.

Your time certainly isn't unlimited. Even the goodwill that you build up by keeping your previous promises to your audience can only go so far. Goodwill is like a bank account; you need to continue to make deposits. Certainly, if you have developed substantial goodwill, your audience will give you the benefit of the doubt when something goes sour—but only for so long. You need to measure performance and investment to make sure that alternative uses for those resources do not drive better results, better sustain your goodwill, and deliver a better return on your investment.

Emerging evaluation metrics

The increased use of social media to deliver messaging has brought with it a range of new, important, and highly effective metrics that help measure the performance of communications efforts. Importantly, you can use these measures and tools to track the impact of programs that were not originally driven via social media. We can separate these measurements into things we need to know before we launch a new program and ways we can measure and adjust the program after it has gone live.

Pre-launch digital metrics

Before we create the first executional idea, we can use these emerging tools to look at the actions of your customers online and the current state of your brand, issue, or policy. This provides a new baseline from which to proceed. Here are a few examples of what you can do to better understand present status, along with key questions you should consider:

- **Search**: The average customer set will make 100 to 150 search engine queries to find out about your brand or topic. Make those queries yourself and see which ones are made most often (look at "results") and which elements of your story or your competitors' stories show up on the first screen. This will provide a bird's eye view of how your audience will learn about you when they are in information-seeking mode.
  - *What will you do to improve your visibility via search?*
- **Keywords:** Visit Google Analytics and enter your brand/topic and related issues. See which words and phrases have the highest volume. You now know which words and phrases your audience is searching

for to find information related to your brand/topic. Remember, if you use the right keywords, you make it easier for your audience to find your story.

> ❑ *Are you using these keywords to tag your content? How often do you use this language in all your content today?*

- **Engagement**: If you look at your existing social media channels (e.g. Facebook, Twitter, Instagram, LinkedIn, etc.), who engages with your content? Who shares, retweets or makes some effort to move your content to their community? These are your power sharers.

> ❑ *How will you engage with your power sharers going forward?*

- **Cross-platform analysis**: If you look at your media coverage, how often does this same media coverage appear in social media channels? If your customers care about your news, they will share it on social media channels.

> ❑ *Are you getting traction or just coverage?*

- **Influencers**: Ask for your media list and see who your organization routinely contacts with news about your brand/topic. How was this list developed? Has it kept pace with the changes in media and in your audience?

> ❑ *Are you reaching the top influencers or just winging it?*

- **Media outlets**: You might be advertising already. Look at your top 150 queries via your Google analysis and see how often each of your target media outlets is showing up in these queries. The good news about search engines is they provide the best way to analyze history. If people like your coverage and they share it, it will show up on the first screen.

> ❑ *How many of your target media outlets are truly impactful, and how many are probably wasteful?*

Traditionally in marketing and advertising, we assumed half of our spend might be wasted. Now, we can see for ourselves the real impact our messages are having. We can know how our audience experiences and shares our story. We can identify the language that matters and whether we're using it or need to brush up on it anew. We know whether engagement is really building momentum in the market. We can readdress who has influence on our brand/topic in terms of people and outlets. We're ready to launch.

Launch digital metrics

Experts have written shelves of books on this topic. (*Digital Marketing Analytics* by Chuck Hemann and Ken Burbary is one of our favorites.) They all espouse a slightly different measurement methodology and provide much more detail for those who want to dive deeper into this facet of evaluation. For our purposes, though, we want to focus on the fundamental metrics that most of those other books include—and that, importantly, are relevant to and useful for any kind of program almost anywhere in the world:

- **First screen progress**: Since you know your baseline for search, you can regularly track the progress you are making, as measured by the move your content makes up the first screen of results for a key query.
    - *Is the experience improving? And is your story showing up in the first two results for each key query? If not, most of your audience will never find your story via mobile.*

- **Language supply chain:** You know which keywords are most important for your audience to find your story. Are you using these keywords in news releases, blog posts, community chats, websites, videos, images, podcasts, and any other content? This type of internal measure is critical to success. It often means that teams inside your organization need to partner for the first time and really work to align metrics.
    - *Are you working as a team across all forms of content to make sure each group's outreach aligns with your audience?*

- **Engagement:** If you run an ad, receive press coverage, or hold an event, you assume this is the start. What happened afterward? Did press coverage lead to conversations on Twitter or Facebook? Did a video on your website gain traction on YouTube? Are images for your topic or brand doing well on Instagram? Are you in constant search to discover whether your audience finds your content relevant, or if they are just being made more aware?

❑ *Are you using cross-platform metrics or still looking at channels in isolation?*

- **Audience architecture:** You need to know who your top influencers are. Who are the 9% of your audience who share your content and who are the key influencers within your 90% world of search. You are building this list continually, ensuring that your team and third-party agencies all contribute to it and sing from the same hymn book. Again, that alignment generates a critical internal improvement to gain external resonance.

  ❑ *What does your list of influencers look like and what is your action plan?*

- **Increasing Precision**: Since online activity can help reveal the subconscious thoughts and behavioral patterns of your audience, you can now look at metrics in a more robust way.

  ❑ *How deeply are you digging into audience data to understand the subtle motivators that nudge them toward the outcome you desire?*

It's worth taking a closer look at some of these more precise measurement capabilities, because they can help you develop more sophisticated communications programs. They also can help you make better adjustments to existing initiatives, so you can continue to deliver a greater return on investment after results from pulling traditional levers diminish.

Conversational metrics show what people say and what they post across virtually every channel, allowing one to identify variations. *Engagement metrics* measure how the same content is shared, and why that might differ from one person or one forum to the next. *Information metrics* track how frequently people search for more information via search engines, revealing what they care about at any particular moment. *Silence metrics* provide an alternative view of that, revealing important cues for why an audience might suddenly stop discussing a topic. And *competitor metrics* reveal what competitors are doing, often revealing what's working or how you might outsmart them.

Because we can see and track our customers' conscious and subconscious actions online, we have a wealth of information to help build insights into their evolution, or lack of evolution, on a given product or issue. And once you dive deep into these metrics, it becomes increasingly clear that *actionable insights* lie within. If data only makes a great Power-Point chart, who cares? If it leads to insights that produce actions or ideas that shape the audience you want to reach, then you are measuring in new ways that make a difference.

After all, as Drucker told us, what gets measured gets managed. As the digital world continues to evolve, the power of the wisdom we gain through evaluation of our execution becomes increasingly evident. In fact, we might even update Drucker to say, "Powerful metrics uncover market truths." It is our job to develop an insights-driven strategy that can be measured, adjusted and constantly improved.

The Three Fundamentals for Measuring Communications Performance

Chuck Hemann
Managing Director, Analytics and Head of Digital Analytics, W2O Group

Measuring marketing and communications performance is consistently at the top of the list of biggest pain points for Chief Marketing Officers (CMO) and Chief Communications Officers (CCO). Almost every third-party study—whether it be from the likes of Deloitte, Gartner or McKinsey—identifies that CMOs and CCOs are investing more heavily than ever in data and analytics. Those studies also tell us that marketing and communications leaders are looking to add more analytics talent to their teams for all kinds of reasons. So, if the CMO and/or CCO is investing in analytics—either through technology, people, or both—then why do these studies articulate that good measurement remains a major challenge? In fact, a 2019 CMO Survey from Gartner indicated that the biggest challenge facing chief marketing officers today is proper measurement.

I think the answer is simpler than the marketing and communications industry thinks. The challenge in doing proper measurement in marketing and communications today isn't technology. The challenge isn't the availability of data. The challenge isn't a lack of talent to conduct proper measurement. The challenge is that our industry has forgotten everything they knew about proper measurement fundamentals. The jury is out on whether that is because of the dizzying array of marketing technology solutions, the number of new channels that exist, or a lot of snake oil salesmen selling metrics like "return on engagement." Regardless of the cause, though, we need to return to the proper measurement fundamentals if we want to reverse the trends found in reports like Gartner's. I believe we need to focus on three important areas:

1. **A good measurement framework focuses less on channels and more on audience progression.** Somewhere during the last 10 years of digital media's growth, we started focusing our measurement on very specific channel key performance indicators (KPIs). That isn't all bad, because we do need a mechanism to optimize and evaluate the performance of specific channels, but marketing programs aren't single channel. Marketing programs are built with the intention of reaching specific audiences on multiple channels and pushing those audiences as far down the funnel as possible. We need to return to developing frameworks with the audience in mind first, then map specific channel KPIs.

2. **Proper planning prevents poor performance.** Remember that old business chestnut? Well, it applies to measurement as well. We spend a significant amount of time planning that "business changing" marketing campaign to make sure it is just right, but only spend a fraction of that time planning the measurement. If the campaign is so "business changing," don't you think the measurement should be just as robust? Companies need to start thinking about benchmarks, technology implications, measurement framework rollout, reporting templates, audiences for reports, etc., and they need to do it far sooner in the process.

3. **Technology is important, but it isn't the savior.** The same Gartner report indicated that approximately 30% of CMOs' budgets are now spent on technology. That seems reasonable, but I think at least part of that spend is done in the hopes that SaaS (Software as a Service) platforms can solve the measurement conundrum for marketing. In my career, I have never seen that happen, and I don't expect that to change any time soon. Good measurement requires a combination of people who understand the business and can translate insights to action.

Will our industry re-focus on the measurement fundamentals so that we stop seeing it on the list of the most frustrating things a CMO needs to deal with? Hopefully so. If not, I fear that marketing budgets will come under greater threat, and those really novel ways of reaching customers through digital channels will go by the wayside. ■

CHAPTER 8

The Power of Persuasion

"Persuasion is often more effectual than force."
—Aesop

Humans have shared entertaining stories since the beginning of time, using narrative to communicate a larger message. Some 2,500 years ago, Aesop created fables to illustrate moral lessons, such as the necessity of invention ("The Crow and the Pitcher," ⬇ **Online Exhibit 8.1**) and why you should look before you leap ("The Fox and the Goat," ⬇ **Online Exhibit 8.2**). By humanizing animals, he made the stories fun and instructive, and he was able to deliver direct messages without offending anyone in power—important, since the man we credit with these tales was a slave.

Every culture has some variation of this type of storytelling that has thrived for centuries, ranging from the Jataka Tales of ancient India to George Orwell's 1945 allegorical novel *Animal Farm*. These stories remind us that we're all the same. Yes, language and culture introduce some level of difference, but the core models of how our brain works are not different. We are wired the same, and we prefer to learn in similar ways.

Back in 500 B.C., we had Aesop to help illustrate shared human strengths and foibles. Today, we have billions of wanna-be Aesops, each moralizing and socializing stories with the help of fiber optic cables, satellite and 5G networks. The result is what late-night talk-show host Stephen Colbert calls the era of "truthiness," which he defines as "the belief in what you feel to be true rather than what the facts will support." Colbert applied the term sarcastically to modern-day politics, but he is not far off from describing how we all tend to think when we are passionate about any topic.

Every day when we go online or turn on the television, we expose our minds to thousands of messages. Our brains are processing content, images, reactions and visual scenes at a rate that would rival a supercomputer. It's impossible to discern exactly what persuades us each and every time. We might say we know, but data science illustrates time and again that the things we tell a researcher often do not match the actions we take. We can, however, study human behavior to understand how our brains work, how we follow patterns, and what those psychological models are all about.

For today's leader, the ability to understand the psychological models that influence an audience is critical to knowing whether a communications effort will achieve its goals. And we have to do this with speed, since the ultimate storytelling platforms, otherwise known as Facebook, Instagram, YouTube and Twitter, are unlocking content—whether true, false or semi-true—in new and innovative ways. When we teach on this subject, Dr. Victoria Romero, chief scientist for Next Century, walks our classes through these models, giving our students deeper insight into the ways humans think, learn and act. What follows in this chapter is the greatest hits version of those models, and a primer for the power of persuasion.

The importance of frequency

The easier we find it to process, understand and remember information, the more likely we are to believe it. Think about this in the context of your organization. Do you create simple messages that avoid the types of jargon that distance you from your audience? Do you get straight to the point or meander? And do you make it easy to remember your campaign? We don't all have an advertising budget the size of Geico's, but we all can ask ourselves: "What's our equivalent of '15 minutes could save you 15 %'?"

In the media world, we have long debated the power of frequency: "To make a decision, does our audience need to see six ads or 10 ads?" Given the speed with which technology is changing, though, these old debates about frequency might be moot. We now live in an age of constancy. We need to break through the noise and, once we do, stay there.

Availability bias

If we see information on an issue with more frequency and recency, we form what experts call "availability bias." For example, we unfortunately hear about gun shootings on a regular basis. This clearly is a major issue, but how likely is it to impact you? Let's put it in perspective: If you combine the annual number of suicides, firearm incidents and motor vehicle deaths, the result is slightly fewer than the total number of deaths due to medical errors that occur each year. If we based our thinking on facts alone, we would be more terrified by the sheer volume of medical errors than the number of shootings. But gun shootings are tragic, often a surprise, receive a lot of media coverage, and capture our attention. Consequently, we become more afraid of a shooting than dying in the hospital of an error, even though the chances of the latter are far greater.

If we spin this idea in a positive direction, availability bias shows us that a regular dialogue with our customers or citizens on topics of mutual interest will help produce greater success. We cannot occasionally reach out to people and hope they remember us. They might, but continual frequency will enhance availability bias, and that fact will change the ways we decide to reach our audiences in the future.

The mere-exposure effect

Often, we believe people with views different from ours hold those divergent opinions because they have a limited view of the world. We assume they've pigeonholed themselves based on what they watch, listen to, or read every day. "Of course they believe that crap," we say, "all they watch is [insert name of that *other* cable channel here]." In reality, we all seek out content that is familiar and predictable, because it soothes us. There is a reason why Aesop's fables have lasted forever. We are comforted when our world makes sense and we are comforted when others repeat ideas and thoughts that match our worldview. This phenomenon is called the mere-exposure effect.

We see the mere-exposure effect play out across almost every facet of our lives. As the famous college football coach Lou Holtz once said: "Never tell your problems to anyone. Twenty percent don't care, and the other eighty percent are glad you have them." But this effect has become far more powerful with the proliferation of media and social media platforms. Using those channels for *narrowcasting*, or playing to a very specific audience, works so well because it builds off the mere-exposure effect. It's easy to disparage narrowcasting—after all, we can see how divisive it can be when reinforcing entrenched political views—but the fact is it works extremely well for selling a product, service, or idea.

To improve your ability to persuade your audience, you need to understand exactly how that audience ticks and why:

- What is the profile of our audience, and are we listening to what they do and say?
- Who does our audience respect? Which topics are most important?
- When are they online or actively consuming content of any type?
- Which people, topics or content are close enough to our audience's worldview that, if introduced, they might expand their knowledge base?

Consider narrowcasting and the mere-exposure effect in terms of a business negotiation, for example. You would never walk into a conference room, state your demands, and then expect the other side to capitulate to your every whim. You study the other side's point of view, you anticipate their questions and arguments, and you walk in with a plan designed for that specific audience—a plan that presents your goals in terms that align with their views. (The folks across the table are going to do the same thing, of course.) These days, the biggest negotiating table is social media. Facebook has 2.2 billion members, and that doesn't even include the subscribers on the Instagram and WhatsApp platforms it owns. That is one big table. What will we say and why? How can we shape the interests of our audience to align more with ours?

Our identities

All humans follow certain patterns. We seek common ground. We think that what we see or hear most often is more important than the rest, whether we believe that information or not. So, how do we shape views and persuade people to take a new action and evolve their perspectives on the world? It's not easy. After all, when we were young we learned that first impressions matter. And while we grow older and (hopefully) more mature, we still condition ourselves to look at someone's appearance and affect to determine who they are—even before they can utter a word.

You see a woman in her early 30s who is well dressed, has shoulder-length hair, is wearing a nice pair of eyeglasses and is holding a sign saying "DACA kids are our kids too." Next to her is a young man in his early 20s in blue jeans and a t-shirt, wearing a semi-smirk and a "Make America Great Again" hat. Some observers might immediately characterize the woman in terms of her career, her views about social issues, and where she lives. Others might assume different things about the young man—where he's from, his level of education, his knowledge of social issues. We have no idea, yet our minds automatically fill in the blanks.

In fairness, we have a lot to evaluate when it comes to forming our own opinions. Our minds are constantly forming first impressions. We develop mild or strong opinions based on our exposure to past content, our interests, and the firehose of new information we encounter every day. Marketers seeking to communicate to their audience and spur them to action need to frame their messages with great care, or risk alienating their target audience and losing the right to have a conversation at all.

Sacred values

If you want to win an argument or move a debate forward, don't focus on sacred values—those values a person will not violate or change for any amount of money, under any circumstances. Importantly, sacred values vary dramatically in different cultures, and what seems absurd or even horrific to one culture is sacred to another. For example, consider the treatment of women in many cultures. From basic freedoms accepted in the West, such as going to school, to the abhorrent concept of honor killing, things we can't fathom are part of the cultural fabric in certain parts of the world.

Sacred values can exist in almost any facet of a person's life. One example closer to most Americans can be found in political discourse about gun control. Imagine trying to persuade an ardent gun owner about the importance of stricter regulations on firearms. If you start out by arguing for a revision of the Second Amendment, you'll likely evoke disgust and anger in those who defend gun ownership as a constitutional right. You will fail to build trust—or damage any trust you might have had—with the audience you hope to persuade. They will stop listening and dig in on their position.

That's how the human brain works. We typically frame arguments in ways that make us feel better, but in so doing often make matters worse. If you frame the debate over gun control in terms of a choice between gun ownership and child welfare, gun advocates will naturally take offense at the suggestion that they don't love their children. The same sentiment expressed in the language of common interest—How can we all work together to make schools safer for our children?—is far more likely to elicit a productive discussion. If we show empathy for our target audience and avoid divisive language, we have a far greater chance of forging a connection. You almost certainly will not change anyone's sacred values, but you might build on other shared values that help sway opinions and produce mutually acceptable solutions.

Similarly, when thinking about communications challenges, it's helpful to contemplate the situation from your counterpart's perspective. Imagine an ad in which Brand A Computer Corp. disses its competitor, listing all the shortcomings of its rival's latest laptop and scoffing at its buttoned-up reputation. At headquarters, the Brand A team feels great; they really stuck it to Brand Z Technologies Inc. But what have they actually gained with their audience? If Brand A is already a customer's favorite computer, you're preaching to the choir. If a customer prefers Brand Z, the ads come across as arrogant, perhaps even offensive. That customer is now more determined than ever to stick with Brand Z. While the folks at Brand A headquarters exchange high-fives and celebrate, their campaign might permanently alienate potential customers. No one likes to hear that their past choices were stupid.

On the other hand, rational fact-based arguments do not change minds on their own, either—even if we, as marketers, often try to convince ourselves that they will. We might list all the ways our product is superior to another, pulling in objective and independently sourced data to support that conclusion. Yet, people aren't purely rational beings. They don't always change their minds, even when presented incontrovertible evidence. Letting people "discover" that your brand works better than aggressively trying to change their minds.

To have any chance of changing minds, your communications and messages need to utilize narratives that make audiences think, help them engage with new people and ideas, and allow them to come to your sought-after conclusion on their own terms. This takes time, as does almost anything worth pursuing. For most people, it's not hard to imagine switching from Apple to Samsung, or to use Netflix less and a new streaming service from Disney more. One might begin to question the rationale of the current government representative and swing to a different candidate in the next election. But in each case, we need to get there ourselves.

Master narratives

In developing your brand positioning, a very useful technique is to take advantage of the "master narratives" of your audience's culture. History serves as a great indicator of what has worked for centuries, even millennia. People prefer to be persuaded, over time, through compelling master narratives—the storylines or themes familiar to everyone in a culture. We tell them over and over again, because they reflect and reinforce our cultural values and group identities. They help us interpret historical and current events so we know how to view ourselves and our place in the world. Like sacred values, master narratives can vary greatly from one culture to another. Most American who hear the phrase "underdog story" immediately understand the key elements of the narrative at hand. When you hear the phrase "star-crossed lovers," you know the plot. If you have been raised in the Middle East in a predominantly Muslim culture, you know the "Crusades" master narrative.

The fight between good and evil and the underdog story are two classic examples. In America, our longstanding mythos around the American Revolution touches on both. The revolution was centered on the idea that colonists would not be oppressed; they would fight back against what was presumed a greater military power and win. The underdogs fighting off the oppressors. The good citizens of the colonies, seeking the great good of freedom, self-rule and democracy, prevailing over the autocratic king an ocean away. We love narratives where good prevails over evil, however we interpret these beliefs. If good hasn't prevailed yet, it's because we aren't done with the story yet. We view character, perseverance, courage and grit as key elements of what makes an underdog into a hero.

In the 2018 election, Beto O'Rourke was viewed as the underdog to incumbent Texas Senator Ted Cruz. His supporters admired his character, his desire to fight for the people, and his charisma as a candidate. They translated these into heroic traits and, while he lost that election, that support eventually catapulted O'Rourke into the 2020 presidential race. That is a powerful underdog-to-hero mentality.

Apple's scrappy early days fostered this same type of narrative, and the company still burnishes that image. People fell in love with the idea that Apple and Steve Jobs were underdogs, pitted against the IBM or Microsoft behemoths. They wouldn't play by the corporate rules, rejecting the traditional conventions for product designs and advertisements in favor of a swagger that permeated the company. That narrative endures, despite its near-bankruptcy in the 1990s, its share of product failures, the passing of Jobs, and now the company's nearly $1 trillion market capitalization. Our beliefs can hold even as an organization evolves—so long as that organization understands its narrative and sticks with it. Apple's narrative never wavered, a rarity in the corporate world.

Master narratives aren't just messages; they're steeped in emotion and history. They carry deeply held characteristics, akin in some ways to our own DNA blueprints. They stick with us forever, and it usually takes a notable external force to cause mutations. The Battle of Karbala took place in the year 61 of the Islamic calendar (680 AD), and it caused a rift among the growing body of Islamic adherents that continues to this day. The conflict pitted a group of supporters and relatives of the prophet Muhammad's grandson, Husayn ibn Ali, and a much larger group of forces of Yazid I, the Umayyad caliph. While Sufi, Sunni and Shia Muslims all view the battle's casualties as martyrs, the fight played a major role in shaping the identity of the Shia, many of whom believe that throughout history their people have been wronged by corrupt and illegitimate regimes.

We realize that 99% of the topics you deal with won't conjure anything close to this sort of intensity. However, utilizing a master narrative in your messaging remains one of the most effective and important methods to persuade. Yet leaders, especially new ones, often overlook the master narratives of the audiences they're trying to reach. This typically happens for two reasons. First, new leaders often discount the history of and around the audience. They arrive filled with new ideas. Whatever happened before was fine, but not nearly as compelling as the ingenious ideas he or she is going to bring to the table. As a result, green leaders seldom undertake a deep dive to understand the actual long-term relationship with their audience. They fail to investigate how they might utilize the master narrative rather than walk away from it. Every brand or organization has characteristics that define it and survive year to year. What are they, and why do they continue to matter? We don't like brands that can't figure out what they are. (You might recall the old Saturday Night Live skit: "It's a dessert topping! It's a floor cleaner. It's both!") A brand that discounts its history unwittingly reveals a lack of clarity about what it really stands for.

Second, new leaders can succumb to "campaignitis," or the inflammation of ideas. We often think of campaigns as unique worlds of their own. If the first campaign doesn't work, well, the second surely will. We'll simply add more ideas and more money. Meanwhile, the audience just wants you to build a better relationship with them, give them more reasons to trust you, and become a more ingrained part of their lives. BMW introduced "The Ultimate Driving Machine" as its global advertising slogan in 1973 and has stuck with it ever since. (⬇ Online Exhibit 8.3) It has become the core brand identity that emphasizes the automaker's dedication to engineering, performance, and the sheer joy of driving its vehicles. Rather than changing their advertising campaign and slogan every few years, as many car makers have over the past half century, BMW has focused on what they want to communicate to aspirational drivers around the world. BMW's outstanding business success and impressive brand equity are testimony to the value of this level of brand discipline.

Identity fusion

When a brand or topic resonates with us, the community around it becomes an extended family. We feel a powerful sense of connection and are willing to make sacrifices for the group and its members. We are often surprised at how an online community will form to protect an individual who is being attacked, or by the way a group will gang up on a company to make a point. Yet, these actions aren't spontaneous and random; they arise because of a group's strong identification with a brand or a cause, whether it be Red Bull-sponsored extreme sports events or Occupy Wall Street.

When we feel a strong identification with a group, our identity begins to fuse with the group's beliefs. As our engagement and our exposure to the messaging increase, our biases are also reinforced. This can lead to amazing success for brands, organizations and issues. We often look at a popular brand and wonder: "Wow, they have a cult-like following." Or we look at a group of people rallying for a cause and ask: "How can they protest in the rain all night long?"

The stuff of fables

Whether we realize it or not, our ability to persuade relies on the under-lying psychology we share as human beings. More-effective persuasion requires an understanding of why people think and act in certain ways, and it asks us to patiently build lasting narratives that drive the best behaviors and actions for our cause. Yes, understanding human psychol-ogy is complex, even for those who spend their careers studying it. We could write an entire series of books about the role of these psychological models on marketing alone. However, even the quick overview provided here underscores just how powerfully persuasive these models can be.

These forces govern our lives and our shared human existence in fun-damental ways. They're part of all of us, and they have been for centuries. They're why the fables endure.

The Wind and the Sun

A dispute once arose between the wind and the sun, which was the stronger of the two, and they agreed to put the point upon this issue, that whichever soonest made a traveler take off his cloak should be accounted the more powerful.

The Wind began, and blew with all his might and main a blast, cold and fierce as a Thracian storm; but the stronger he blew the closer the traveler wrapped his cloak around him, and the tighter he grasped it with his hands.

Then broke out the Sun. With his welcome beams he dispersed the vapor and the cold; the traveler felt the genial warmth, and as the Sun shone brighter and brighter, he sat down, overcome with the heat, and cast his cloak on the ground.

Thus the Sun was declared the conqueror, and it has ever been deemed that persuasion is better than force; and that the sunshine of a kind and gentle manner will sooner lay open a poor man's heart than all the threatening and force of blustering authority.

That's a valuable moral of the story for all of us who want to be effective communicators.

How to Persuade a Tough Audience

Mike Linton
Enterprise Chief Marketing Officer at Farmers Insurance Group of Companies

One of the key communication challenges many of us in business will eventually (if not often) face is trying to persuade a skeptical audience that has a negative opinion of a category, brand, or issue. If you look back in recent history, there are many examples:

- American automobiles were viewed as generally inferior to many imports

- Quick service restaurants (QSRs) came to be viewed as unhealthy

- Cable companies and many airlines developed reputations for poor customer service

- Many technology companies are viewed as putting profits ahead of privacy

- Then there's the super tough challenge—marketing to an opposing political party

All these are "tough audiences" of people who start with the presumption that they don't need to hear your side of the story. They have already made up their mind. If you are trying to persuade them to your point of view by simply repeating your arguments as to why they should agree with you—sorry, no soup for you!

So, here are three tactics for dealing with and eventually persuading those tough audiences:

1. **Admit the issue exists:** If consumers think fast food is unhealthy, United doesn't care about customers, Jaguars break down a lot, or my hometown of Cleveland, Ohio, wouldn't be any fun to visit, telling them they are wrong won't change their minds. It will probably just make them even more convinced they are right. You have to first understand why they feel that way and look for their kernels of truth. It is critical to acknowledge to yourself that, many times, their opinions are legitimate. If you dismiss tough audiences as irrational or use the words "they just don't understand us," you have no chance of winning them over. How many times has a Republican or Democrat converted an opponent by pointing out the errors of their thinking? My guess is never.

2. **Talk in their language:** If you think my product is too expensive, telling you it isn't too expensive won't change your mind. I need to show you

why my product value is worth the money, either by changing your perspective ("Isn't your skin worth an extra dollar a day?"); showing you my product has changed ("New and improved taste!"); or reducing your risk of giving us a try (free samples and money back guarantees). The customer is processing your marketing message on their terms with their own logic. Your job is to understand what part of their logic and feelings is blocking the sale, then solve for that issue. Your job is not to insist your logic is right. Don't try to shortchange the entire process by claiming the "tough problem has now gone away." For example, changing your brand name while leaving the basic business as is doesn't really solve anything—that's like thinking a fresh coat of paint will fix your home's foundation problems. (I'm looking at you Time Warner Cable...I mean Spectrum!)

3. **Acknowledge this is a journey, not a single step:** Think of all the times you have changed your mind on a product, a person, or a political idea. Maybe that has come in a blinding flash: "Hey, Comcast is great at service and worth every penny! United really does love to fly! Google does care about my privacy!" More likely, it takes time and a series of positive customer experiences. Remember, you are rewiring the logic of an individual, not selling into a vacuum. That will usually take a gradual, consistent approach, so don't count on catching lightning in a bottle. Slow and steady wins this race.

Don't be discouraged if you don't "win the argument" with a tough audience in the first round. If you demonstrate you understand where they are coming from, speak in their language, and recognize that dialogue takes time, you're already in a much better place. Tough times and arguments don't always last, but smart communicators can and do. And they often achieve more than most folks thought was ever possible—even persuading a tough audience to embrace their point of view—if they do it in a smart, strategic, and consistent manner. ■

CHAPTER 9

Connecting with Youth

"Children learn as they play. Most importantly,
in play children learn how to learn."
—O. Fred Donaldson

"I really love being human.
But some days I really wish I could be a fairy."
—Greta, age 4

From the beginning of time, parents—and adults in general—have struggled to understand children. We wonder how their interests and concerns, their habits and values, can be so very different from ours. There's nothing more perplexing than figuring out how to reach them—whether we're talking about, teenagers, Gen Z, or millennials.

Of course, it is no surprise that young people see the world with a different mindset and through a different lens than our own. We scratch our heads as kids listen endlessly to their peers describe how to play a video game via their favorite YouTube channel. We're startled to realize that our picture is being taken for today's Snapchat story. The list goes on. What might be more amazing is that we seem to have forgotten how our parents viewed us.

The good news is that all humans' brains develop in the same way and are guided by the same instincts. Over time, technology and a range of other external factors introduce differences as they shape who we become. But the basic building blocks of the human mind are the same, whether you're born in Helena, Montana, or Hyderabad, India, or Harare, Zimbabwe.

While not all businesses, startups, nonprofits, and government departments and agencies have a specific interest in persuasive communication with young audiences, enough of us do that we believe this segment deserves special attention. For many of the organizations we have taught at the U.S. Marketing Communication College (USMCC), reaching young people is critical. Some are challenged with inoculating young people against the hateful messaging that eventually leads to violent extremism. Others strive to share the opportunities that a great education in the United States provides. Still others seek to provide the facts on which youth in other countries might base decisions about their futures, but to which they have little or no access in their home environments. Understanding how young people think and learn and interact with the world is essential to all these efforts.

Appreciating how their thinking and brain chemistry evolve over time is equally important. How you engage with young people varies dramatically depending on their stage of development. This chapter takes a topline look at how children and adolescents develop and how to take this into account when creating an ABCDE model. This information is based on the work of Nancy Zwiers, one of our talented faculty members who spent most of her career marketing to children in the toy and entertainment industries with companies including Disney, Mattel, and Spin Master.

The global generation

The explosion of social media and the continued impact of pop culture around the world has produced a globally connected generation of young people. Disney Channels Worldwide span 160 countries and 30 different languages. *The Avengers* movie earned $1.5 billion in theaters around the world. *Iron Man* raked in $1.2 billion. *Frozen* was produced in 41 languages, and two-thirds of its $1.3 billion in box office revenue came from outside the United States. About 12 million gamers globally play World of Warcraft online, and every day more than 30 million viewers—many of them in their teens—watch the YouTube videogame commentaries produced by a 29-year-old Swede named Felix Arvid Ulf Kjellberg. Only they all know him as PewDiePie.

The sheer diversity of these audiences around the globe is amazing to behold. Yet, even more noteworthy is the fact that youth around the world are more the same than perhaps any other time in history. While it's important to remain sensitive to certain geographical and cultural differences, our past assumptions about reaching this audience might need to change.

Young, emotional brains

As we begin our lives, we see the world primarily through an emotional lens. Over time we mature, but young people make decisions in a very different way during this period than when they are fully formed adults.

- Unconscious vs. Conscious
- Here and Now Focus vs. Future
- Take Action vs. Consider Actions
- Heart vs. Head
- Concrete vs. Abstract
- Visual vs. Verbal
- "Does it feel good?" vs. "Does it make sense?"

Young, emotional brains are playful—regardless of generation, geography, or culture. Your parents went through these stages. So did your great-grandparents. No matter where or when they were born or raised, they experienced the world this way. These features of young minds arise from an inner drive to learn. It is nature's way of teaching. And while they exert the strongest influence on the young, they last in some form throughout everyone's lifetime.

How the brain forms

This isn't a neuroscience tutorial, but it is important to understand a few of the basics as they apply to our model. The majority of human brain formation occurs between birth and age 25. We are certainly capable of continuing to learn, but by age 25 our brains are already wired with memories, habits and experiences—both good or bad—that stick with us for life. This is why we still love the same music we listened to in high school. It is why we fall in love with brands or ideas all over again when companies re-introduce them in a "retro" fashion. Strong memories die hard.

From a communications standpoint—whether you are marketing a soft drink or instilling a value of multiculturalism—the earlier we can help create memories, moments, and other positive and long-lasting experiences, the more likely we are to earn the trust and respect of youth for the long haul. Sometimes, that can last a lifetime. So how do we do that?

Core play patterns

Researchers note that virtually every child learns through play, so naturally children's play patterns can tell us a great deal about how they come to think about the world around them. This type of playful learning passes through four distinct stages: exploration and discovery, challenge and mastery, imitation role play, and empowerment fantasies. If your audience includes children, teens, and young adults, understanding these phenomena can help you craft better communication strategies and executions.

Exploration and discovery

Beginning in infancy, children experience excitement from anticipation and the thrill of the hunt. Young children are discovering things for the very first time and storing those experiences. They crave novelty. This is a time of self-discovery, whether it's noticing their toes for the first time or playing peek-a-boo. They love surprises.

This innate behavior drives infants to explore the environment around them. As they grow older, the pattern extends beyond the physical environment to everything from verbal interaction to reading—skills not necessary for survival, but certainly beneficial. At every step of exploration and discovery, the patterns are inherent in virtually every child. These instinctive behaviors are consistent across cultures.

This delight in discovery doesn't stop as we age, of course. How many times have you taken an online quiz or filled out a chart in a magazine to find out which superhero you would most likely be? We tap into our innate child-like impulses throughout our lives.

Challenge and mastery

Also from infancy, people enjoy gameplay, challenging themselves and engaging in various forms of competition—either solo or as a member of a team. Challenge and mastery can be physical, emotional or cognitive. And progression through levels of achievement can make this factor addictive.

"Gamification" is the application of game mechanics to non-game activities and processes to both engage and motivate an audience. As a child, you might have played games to get points as a means of measuring success. As an adult, you might collect Starbucks points or frequent-flier miles to attain some reward. When you need to choose among comparably priced airlines, you might select one over the others because it gives you more miles, perks, or recognition. Have you become a devotee of products like Fitbit? Do you keep track of your steps just for your own interest, or do you compete with peers, siblings, neighbors?

Gameplay taps into the internal compulsion to master something. The achievement you seek could be meeting the challenge itself, or it might be a valued reward. For some, the motivation is simply the competitive desire to surpass another or to attain a personal best. For others, it is a matter of status and recognition. And for still others it is simply a means of self-expression.

Through challenge and mastery, children start to seek things outside their comfort zone and core environment. They begin to expand their knowledge and skills through external experiences, such as sports and game play.

Imitation role play

From our very first moments, we learn by mimicking others. In the beginning, our models tend to be parents and siblings. As we get older, they extend outward to include what we see in our community, movies, or social media. The science behind these actions is the mirror neuron system. Mirror neurons are activated by watching others, and we model the behaviors we observe. As we do so, these mirror neurons form the seat of our human empathy. We relate when we see others' emotions, and emotions can be contagious.

Entertainment is a key facet of this stage. As entertainment becomes more interactive, the lines between entertainment and play begin to blur. Children soon imitate the characters or role models they admire. As adults, these models may morph from fantasy characters to real-life celebrities, sports figures, and even peers.

Empowerment Fantasies

Discussions of empowerment fantasies have drawn critical responses from some of our students during our Marketing College sessions because they perceived our lessons as reinforcing gender stereotypes. In fact, what researchers have found in relation to children's empowerment fantasies very much resemble the dominant gender stereotypes in most global cultures. Yet, understanding those innate trends is one way to better understand and address how they play out in our children's and our own lives.

But let's make one thing clear: A wealth of objective, scientific research supports this discussion. We are reporting, not judging or endorsing. Furthermore, we are talking about broad trends, so exceptions absolutely exist. If what follows doesn't fit with your world view, feel free to disregard it, but we do urge you to understand the science behind this before you reject it out of hand.

Empowerment fantasies drive most play patterns among children, and they are fundamental to gender identity. They are most extreme from ages 3 through 6, and then moderate thereafter. In general, males are *valiant or violent*, while females are *nurturing and empowering*. (Figure 9.1)

FIGURE 9.1
Empowerment fantasies compared

Heroic Fantasy	Nurturing Fantasy
In the heroic fantasy, it is important to be *brave*. Think of the superheroes that are most attractive to young boys.	In the nurturing fantasy, it is important to be *loving*. Think of the traditional Disney princesses and what matters to them.
The battle is between good and evil. Typical scenarios include cops and robbers or humans versus aliens.	Here the desire is not to do battle at all but rather to rescue, nurture, and befriend.
The goal is to vanquish evil.	The goal is to convert evil to good.
This is an unabashedly competitive mindset. Winning. Keeping score.	This is much more cooperative.
Friends have a clear power hierarchy. There is an alpha who is followed.	Friends are equals. But this can often lead to conflict.
This fantasy is more action-oriented.	This fantasy is more verbally oriented.

The Youth Marketer's Toolbox

As a marketer, you can and should take advantage of the internal motivations behind these play patterns:

- **Exploration and Discovery:** Children are curious. How can you use that? They love surprises. How can you use that? Perhaps you can build a quiz into your messaging to help it stick.
- **Challenge and Mastery:** There are opportunities for gamification. Competitions. Points. Leaderboards. Rewards and acknowledgement for achievement. Sports is a universal interest. How can you engage youth through sports and competitions?
- **Imitation Role Play:** Behavior modeling is a powerful tool. How might you interact with your audience to curry a desired behavior?

■ **Empowerment Fantasies:** Be careful about imposing your own value system as you present the heroic and nurturing fantasies. While there are certainly exceptions, ask yourself whether your target is a broad audience or a specific subset.

The adolescent brain

Up to now, we've largely been talking about the development of the brain during the early years. These patterns continue into the formative teenage years, albeit in a somewhat more sophisticated form. What we begin to see is a set of concerns common to teenagers of all stripes. As mentioned earlier, our brains are more or less developed by the time we are 25 years old. But during adolescence our gray matter is still, in a sense, under construction.

In adults, rational thinking is driven by the prefrontal cortex, a region of the brain that is still in development during our teens, leaving us to rely on the amygdala to help form decisions. Unfortunately, the amygdala is the "bad angel" on our shoulder, manifesting itself emotionally, aggressively and impulsively. Most people survive their amygdala-inspired foolishness and develop the neurological capacity to handle complex planning, risk assessment and decision-making, but these turbulent teenage years offer a window for us to reach youth with messages that may resonate for life.

Impulse control

Impulse control originates in the prefrontal cortex. Self-control develops gradually through childhood and adolescence, peaks in adulthood and then declines as we enter old age. (Figure 9.2) As you have observed pre-teens and teens, you have probably wondered, "When are they going to grow up?" This isn't a matter of teens just deciding to be out of control. Their brains haven't gotten them there yet.

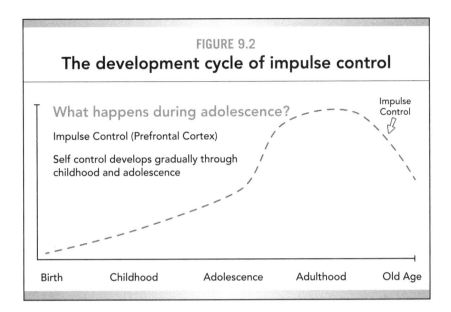

FIGURE 9.2
The development cycle of impulse control

What happens during adolescence?

Impulse Control (Prefrontal Cortex)

Self control develops gradually through childhood and adolescence

Impulse Control

Birth Childhood Adolescence Adulthood Old Age

Emotions

Emotions dominate the decision-making of children and young adolescents. The emotion centers of the brain connect to the decision centers before the logic and reasoning centers can. Emotions, while never disappearing, of course, begin to take a back seat to logic and reasoning as we age. (Figure 9.3)

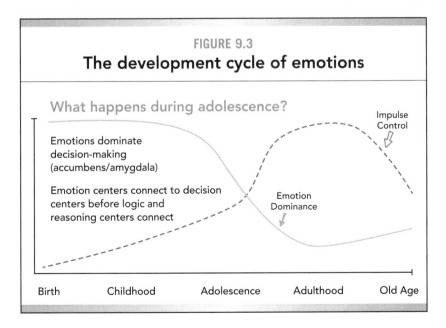

FIGURE 9.3
The development cycle of emotions

What happens during adolescence?

Impulse Control

Emotions dominate decision-making (accumbens/amygdala)

Emotion centers connect to decision centers before logic and reasoning centers connect

Emotion Dominance

Birth Childhood Adolescence Adulthood Old Age

Reward circuits

Reward seeking is a strong drive during the adolescent years. (Figure 9.4) Risks actually become very attractive. That's why telling a young person not to do something because it is dangerous can be counterproductive. Trying to dissuade young people from drag racing with friends or joining the jihad or even the U.S. military because it is dangerous could prod them to do the opposite.

Peer affiliation

The need for peer affiliation and intimacy increases dramatically in early adolescence and then plateaus. (See Figure 9.4) It never really goes away. You can see how the appeals of risk and reward, supported by the need for peer acceptance, combine before impulse control can moderate decisions.

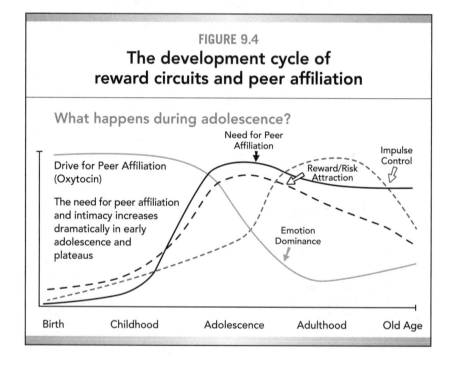

FIGURE 9.4
The development cycle of reward circuits and peer affiliation

What happens during adolescence?

Need for Peer Affiliation

Impulse Control

Drive for Peer Affiliation (Oxytocin)

Reward/Risk Attraction

The need for peer affiliation and intimacy increases dramatically in early adolescence and plateaus

Emotion Dominance

Birth | Childhood | Adolescence | Adulthood | Old Age

Logic and reasoning

The prefrontal cortex catches up as we move from adolescence to adulthood. (Figure 9.5) Eventually the brain begins to allow logic to impact other aspects of the decision matrix. If you are trying to make a logical case to persuade children and young adults to do anything, you are pushing water uphill.

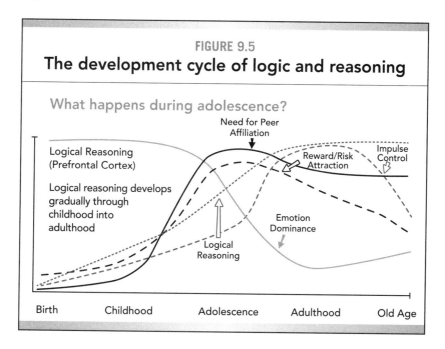

FIGURE 9.5
The development cycle of logic and reasoning

What happens during adolescence?

The net effect

The net effect

Not surprisingly, this combination of typical brain-development patterns make the turbulent and formative years a unique period for companies and organizations hoping to persuade youth. (Figure 9.6) Whether trying to interest them in a video game or convincing them of the value of public service, engaging with teens requires a focus on emotion over logic, and understanding of impulse control (or lack thereof), the role their peers play in their lives, and their higher inclination toward risk. Combine that with the greater independence they're starting to enjoy, and you can easily see how they present a unique and important audience for well-planned communication.

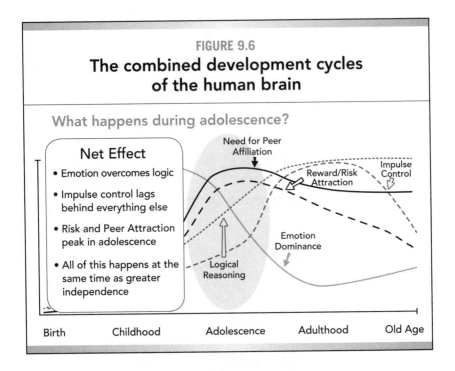

FIGURE 9.6

The combined development cycles of the human brain

What happens during adolescence?

Net Effect

- Emotion overcomes logic
- Impulse control lags behind everything else
- Risk and Peer Attraction peak in adolescence
- All of this happens at the same time as greater independence

Need for Peer Affiliation

Reward/Risk Attraction

Impulse Control

Emotion Dominance

Logical Reasoning

Birth   Childhood   Adolescence   Adulthood   Old Age

The marketing connection

From infancy, we're hardwired to learn how to play and explore. Play is a biological drive originating from the inside. Entertainment, on the other hand, moves from the outside in. We receive content, process it, and decide what to make of it. Both processes have immense value for youth, but each emerges from different sources and works differently.

Play is nature's way of ensuring we learn what we need to survive. It's fueled by curiosity and the satisfaction and thrill we find in discovery. No matter your generation, we have all learned in remarkably similar ways, even if the source of our entertainment has changed over the years. Baby Boomers watched cartoons on Saturday morning, choosing from three channels. If you're among that generation, you might have loved *Speed Racer* and *Jonny Quest*. If you missed them in the morning, you had no on-demand options. But hey, you didn't know any better. You went outside to play and made up your own games with the neighborhood kids.

Today, many youth around the world are growing up with a panoply of high-tech options. They can record shows or watch them on-demand.

They can choose digital or physical play, but either way they can immerse themselves in a game, whether online or in the backyard. Children today expect to be able to customize almost any kind of play situation.

Mobile phones are everything

Every day, approximately 300,000 people are born. They will speak one of 8,300 languages that exist on earth. Ten of those languages reach 82 % of people online, mostly through mobile phones. On average in the United States, kids get their first cell phone at age 10, according to a 2016 survey by Influence Central. A study by the International Central Institute for Youth and Educational Television found that 88 % of children in Germany have a smartphone by age 12. In South Korea, nearly three-quarters of 10- to 12-year-olds own a smartphone, according to a 2016 report in the journal *Computers in Human Behavior*.

Youth will treat this phone as the center of their universe for the rest of their lives. What can stream into a phone is what will shape them, which means things made of paper (e.g., newspapers or magazines) or content that requires planning to view (e.g., TV shows) will not make the cut. Children live in a world where content that goes to social makes the difference. They don't have to come get the content; it comes to them when and where they want it.

In most countries, Facebook is the central platform for TV, updates, and general learning. Think of this trend as "TV to social." Though you may hear in some western countries that Facebook is not as popular as it once was, the rest of the world hasn't gotten that memo. Instagram and WhatsApp, both of which Facebook owns, are very popular throughout the world, as is YouTube. Google, which owns YouTube, is the primary search engine. The other channels we are familiar with, such as Twitter, Pinterest and Snapchat, are important in large western countries, but their reach drops considerably when you look at global scale. We can expect Facebook, with a community of billions, to keep setting the pace for years to come.

When we think of our audience, we should ask ourselves which channels and outlets are most effective at reaching our target segment. We should stop asking questions like "How can I get more youth to tune into our show?" Instead, we should be asking, "How can I effectively transmit this TV segment to our audience via Facebook or YouTube?" The key theme no longer centers around a "please visit us" scenario; now, the key theme is "how do I reach you?"

Youth seldom rely on just one online channel, so it's important that we think of media and metrics across multiple platforms. Stories and experiences will disseminate over multiple channels. But the good news is that humans are still humans: We rarely use more than four channels on a daily basis. You can apply all these findings into the creation of more effective communication campaigns when you have a young target audience. (See Box 9.1)

BOX 9.1
Marketing rules of thumb for young audiences

Rely on stories rather than facts and figures: Tell a story rather than trying to win your audience over with facts and statistics. One reason that stories work better than statistics is that we innately respond to the human scale. A picture of one starving child has significantly more impact than a chart that illustrates the suffering of thousands. A second reason is that we are wired to respond to a narrative that has a beginning, a middle and an end. Pixar movies follow a tried-and-true formula. You can fill in the blanks for any of their fabulously successful films:

Once upon a time there was a [_____]. Every day, [_____].

One day, [_____]. Because of that, [_____].

Because of that, [_____]. Until finally [_____].

Consider using humor or celebrities to convey your message: Humor can be a powerful tool, even when the subject is serious. Sometimes it makes the topic easier to absorb. Use your judgment; humor isn't always appropriate for your message. Celebrities can help you break through the noise, and children find them compelling.

Social media can help you build a movement: Take advantage of the bandwagon that can grow very quickly on social media. The Red Nose Day program is a great example of an event that went viral and, to date, has raised nearly $150 million to help end child poverty. The ALS Ice Bucket Challenge took on a very serious issue, Lou Gehrig's disease, and made it into a global cause via sharing on social media. (The humor of having a bucket of ice dumped on your head and the many celebrity participants certainly helped, as well.)

Show, don't tell: Use visuals to tell your story. A headline that argues your point might not get as much attention as a powerful visual. Using an arresting image with the right copy can make a bigger impact. The United Nations developed a powerful message with print ad for women's rights, simply using a woman's face with her mouth covered by a Google search box that said, "A woman shouldn't." (⬇ Online Exhibit 9.1) When you do use only words, be pithy. Nike didn't need to say anything more than "Just Do It" for its iconic ad campaign. (⬇ Online Exhibit 9.2)

Leverage peer-to-peer communication. Help your audience connect with your message at a human level. Your competition does this very well. Terrorist organizations have become extremely adept at using interaction between peers to sway youth toward extremist causes. They no longer rely on traditional images of heavily armed, masked men, hiding out in deserts or jungles. In fact, one terror recruitment effort featured an entire series of cat videos, including a young man holding his cat and looking anything but sinister. (⬇ Online Exhibit 9.3)

Play on the power of music. Anthropologists theorize that the universality of music traces to its role in emotional regulation and social bonding. Take advantage of this innate opportunity.

The future is now

More and more, brands will have to accommodate new uses of technology in their messaging. For the last few years, Bob and his now 23-year-old daughter, Brittany, have written a series of blog posts titled "Millennials Unplugged" (⬇ Online Exhibit 9.4), which explores what is next for the world of marketing. Here is what they are learning and what some key takeaways are:

Advertising will become highly interactive and more personal as attention spans decrease

We can already see this in the rise of the six-second ad. Ads scroll as you move onscreen. You can learn whether a brand you like and want to buy is available nearby and at what price. It will become normal for ads to interact with us, teach us what to do, and show us where to go to complete a purchase. The days of advertising simply to generate awareness are ending.

  - **Key takeaway:** We decide within one to three seconds whether we will watch a video on Facebook, follow a story on Snapchat, or listen to a song on Pandora. Our advertisements and stories need to match these limited attention spans. The good news is that once we get the attention of anyone, including youth, they will hang in there and listen to the remainder of the story. In a sense, it's similar to the inverted pyramid used by journalists—start with the main point and work your way steadily down to less impactful material from there.

The user experience will drive the device or channel we target with our ads

Media planners will study what customers do online, very nearly in real time, and then serve up the appropriate interactive experiences on any device or through any medium that provides content. The best marketing pros will identify and understand audience behavior clearly enough to integrate a brand story into the user experience without it coming across as more promotional chatter. Youth won't care if these interactions occur while they are watching TV from their phones, streaming satellite radio, or texting with friends, as long as it is relevant and not disruptive.

  - **Key takeaway:** Red Bull is the undisputed leader in understanding how to integrate a story and their brand into an immersive experience, sponsoring an array of extreme sports and unique events. Whether we are watching the X Games or viewing daredevil skydiver Felix Baumgartner's historic jump from space, we don't mind being entertained by a brand if it aligns with our interests. The results speak for themselves. Red Bull almost crashed YouTube's servers when more than 8 million viewers attempted to watch Baumgartner's 2012 jump simultaneously.

For e-commerce, the ability to buy will match our timing and desire to buy

Buy buttons will become a part of every social channel we use. Customers will expect to interact with a brand on their schedule, so following multiple clicks to find an online point of sale will feel prehistoric. They will decide to buy when they feel like it, and do it with relative ease, whether via a social channel, app, search result, or messaging service. Their social layer becomes the next retail frontier.

- **Key takeaway:** We have always known that with each extra click we build into making a purchase, we lose customers. That's why Amazon offers one-click purchasing as an option. Streamlining the e-commerce experience will allow people to view posts on Facebook and contribute to a cause or buy the coat they like without leaving the site. If your audience enjoys the experience you offer, they are ready for action.

We will present data that fits the situation and the device

Completion rates for vertically oriented video ads are nine times higher than for horizontally oriented ads. (Think of printing out a picture in portrait/vertical or landscape/horizontal mode.) Content—whether earned, shared, owned, or paid—must fit the nuanced usage patterns of the devices customers prefer. We have worried for too long about where an ad will show up on a website or search page. Now, the important factor is not just where the ad shows up, but how. A horizontal ad signals a company mired in old-school thinking, not thinking of a predominately smartphone carrying audience. It's a small detail, and one that's easy to fix, but left uncorrected these sorts of oversights can antiquate your brand image.

- **Key takeaway:** Going from horizontal to vertical is a basic move. There is another reason why we need this full screen—on mobile phones, it provides a fuller image to better illustrate and narrate life.

The people most successful at building YouTube audiences have a remarkable ability to show humanity in all its messiness and glory. Anthony Gaetano, known as "Ant," has 1.9 million subscribers on YouTube. In his 10- to 20-minute daily video segments, Ant doesn't just show viewers how to use Roblox, he fills their smartphones with life.

Messaging apps will become more powerful than email

Messaging apps have always made the crowd more informed and, hopefully, a little smarter. Email doesn't allow the sort of crowdsourcing that can give us greater insights. Messaging apps also facilitate conversations that won't clog up an inbox. As youth are already figuring out, both personally and professionally, we can use improved messaging apps not just to share relevant content faster, but to narrow the group of recipients to those participating in the conversation. Throw your pre-formatted distribution lists away. We'll work in a world where we might have 10 messaging apps, all integrated, that keep us in the loop with the right teams. Youth will lead us there.

- **Key takeaway:** If we look at WhatsApp (owned by Facebook) or WeChat (developed by Tencent), we can see how two of the most powerful companies on earth are redefining messaging. These apps now integrate video, audio, e-commerce, digital payments, and more. Basically, the companies and their users view messaging as the central platform of the future, not an adjunct. This revolution is powerful, radical and happening right in front of us.

Collaboration will improve as we use live streaming, game-type formats, and better visuals to solve problems

A pilot can sit in an office in Nevada and command a drone in Afghanistan. Gamers can play Fortnite at any time with friends anywhere in the world. The ability to visualize data, gamify it, and make it relevant to business will lead to new ways of solving the most intractable commercial problems. We will achieve as a worldwide team what we can't achieve via software alone. Software as a Service (SaaS) will never be able to do what humans can do in partnership with it.

- Key takeaway: Augmented reality (AR) can already deliver on its promise to superimpose content—sounds, images, and text—on our natural world. Depending on what we care about, we'll be able to look at a bag of coffee and, via our phone or other AR device, see where it was produced and by whom. Or we might look at a bicycle and instantly learn all about its specifications and customer reviews. Once again, experience moves front and center.

Brands that curate value from user-generated content will become more effective in the market

Snapchat brilliantly culls through the best of its user-generated content and then shares it so other users can get updates on a city or event. Brand managers used to accumulate all that knowledge themselves and employ it to create their own ideas and campaigns. Now, they can identify important emerging content, curate it, and skillfully share it with their audience in real time. It's faster, and it tends to embody a greater authenticity than 99 % of the content companies produce. We don't know what the job title will end up being, but we will soon see the equivalent of "content curator" on job posting sites.

- **Key takeaway:** The next big idea might be easier than you think. Remember the famous Oreo dunk during the 2013 Super Bowl? Well, fast-forward to 2016, and Gatorade upped the game. They built an animated filter on Snapchat, which allowed users to dunk a virtual Gatorade cooler over other users' video selfies. Only a single "G" was shown. They achieved 160 million impressions during a game watched by 115 million. Not bad. Again, experience-driven.

The Internet of Things is accepted as a way to reach technological integration in our lives

Youth want to get smarter, and they are comfortable letting sensors and algorithms monitor what they do to help them gain knowledge and create a better experience. As long as they get smarter and their experience improves, few will care that a brand unobtrusively integrated its message into the interaction. We can put in any sensors we want and use beacons or other mechanisms to track behavior if we provide more value in return—and if we don't just use this as a method to more directly sell products. This is a very thin line; marketers who don't get this right will be slammed and shut down.

- ■ **Key takeaway:** It is becoming the new normal to wear a fitness device of some type. We like to learn about ourselves, so we're also making ourselves and our data part of the experience journey. That will only increase as we add sensors to our clothing and shoes and start to aggregate this knowledge.

Some things stay the same

In their "Millennials Unplugged" series, Brittany and Bob emphasize that we need to approach our efforts to learn about youth with the same rigor that we use to approach machine learning, search, or any other aspect of marketing. Once you do, it is revealing to see the differences and similarities between youth and "the rest of us."

Big screens can still win: When we're going to sit down for 90 minutes and watch something, the comfy seat and a bigger screen will always be more fun. Some things don't change even with technology. Movie theaters are still cool to visit.

Who knows what youth may be thinking about, though: They are always on a second or third device while watching TV. Basically, no matter what is on the big screen, something is competing for their attention on the small screen.

Being in the moment matters: A positive aspect of short attention spans is that youth like to be in the moment.

Youth define "friends" differently: In today's Facebook world, many millennials have between 500 and 2,000 friends, many of whom were originally friends of friends. These associations are leading to much larger friend groups that often include classmates, teams, companies, and other groups. The good news, from a parent's perspective, is that youth do seem to want to know their friends; they don't let just anyone in, and they rarely meet someone for the first time via Facebook.

New dialects and languages are being created right in front of us: The auto-correct smartphone feature has helped spawn a common slang. Just as Google knows what we are typing in when we search and Gmail will suggest how to finish your sentence, phones increasingly anticipate our intentions. The future will have a new mashup of text short-hand, emojis, and native language. This development could potentially make it easier for youth to reach their peers worldwide and start to tear down the natural barrier of language. It also means that the brands that don't constantly renovate how they speak will sound increasingly out of date. Understanding this language is just as important as ferreting out the words driving search, since the languages of text and search are becoming one.

The bottom line for reaching a youth audience

It's important to understand that all the fundamentals discussed throughout this book apply to youth. There is no separate ABCDE model for young audiences. However, to reach youth effectively, three big trends can make all the difference:

1. The mobile phone is the center of their universe.

2. The experience matters.

3. Attention spans are shorter than the time it took you to read this sentence.

Studying how youth are learning and evolving worldwide has instilled in us a deep respect for the importance of understanding where your audience is and how they consume content, what behaviors they exhibit and why, and which channels and outlets they prefer. We are changing our metrics to capture these subtle yet seismic changes.

Five Core Truths about Innovation

Doug Hall
Founder, Eureka! Ranch, Innovation Engineering and
Brain Brew Custom Whisk(e)y

After helping to create and test more than 25,000 innovations and enable the commercialization of $17 billion in innovation valuation, I've learned the following five things are critical to success.

1. **Align on what an innovation is at the start:** We define an idea as an innovation if it is "meaningfully unique." We measure it by asking customers how likely they are to purchase (meaningfulness) and how new and different (unique) they perceive the idea to be. With meaningful uniqueness as the definition, innovation is no longer a debate. Rather, it's grounded in factual evidence. And it works. Ideas with greater meaningful uniqueness create word of mouth, awareness, distribution trial purchase/usage and repeat purchase/usage.

2. **Failure is fundamental:** Meaningfully unique innovations are those that have never been done before. To make them real, you need to test, try and experiment. You must embrace failure as just the normal process required to turn big ideas into reality. Rapid cycles of experimentation are run because we don't know the answer before we begin. Importantly, these cycles of learning are not random. Rather, they are disciplined iterations of what is known as the Deming cycle—Plan, Do, Study, Act. Importantly, "study" is used in place of "check" in the cycles.

3. **No math, no innovation:** Doing the math on sales, savings, profits, costs, etc., turns your idea into a business opportunity. Doing the math helps you make sure that your idea has the potential to make a meaningful difference in the world. When you do the math using the new risk-adjusted methods, you quickly quantify the areas of greater risk due to uncertainty in your understanding.

4. **No patent, no innovation:** The highest standard of meaningful uniqueness is an innovation that is patentable. Ideas that are patentable generate pride and passion. Ideas that are patentable are, by definition, non-obvious to someone with ordinary skill in the area. Conversely, ideas that are not patentable are obvious. Sadly, existing patent writing, searching and management systems are not aligned to the newest laws and best practices. In fact, when we give business leaders our patent

literacy test, they score 60% correct. Note that because it's a true/false test, 50% correct would be random guessing.

5. **You gotta LOVE it:** If you don't love—and I mean *really* love—your innovation, then you're not going to invest the energy required to make it happen. Innovation equals change, and working through change requires a massive investment of energy. The only way you can sustain the energy required to commercialize a meaningfully unique idea is if you really love it. ■

CHAPTER 10

Digital Marketing

> **"We shape our dwellings, and afterwards
> our dwellings shape us."**
> −Winston Churchill

The days of pushing out a message and praying that it works are over. Technology is revolutionizing marketing, just as it's revolutionizing our world. But as we've witnessed repeatedly over the years, people often feel overwhelmed when faced with this brave new world. If you are a policy expert, a small-business entrepreneur, or a music producer, why would you be an expert in marketing, much less digital marketing?

Most people default to one of three ways of dealing with the ceaseless wave of emerging innovation. There are the status quo champions, who remind us of how successful we've been in the past and the "fact" that we already know what to do. We have the avoidance experts, who listen intently and ask questions but never dip a toe in the water and actually make a decision. And we have the other extreme, the Steve Jobs disciples, who want to absorb all ideas with the spirit that one of them will succeed. None of these approaches works well.

The good news is that you don't have to be a superhero to figure out the best way to do marketing in this digital world. Put the cape away and just focus on the fundamentals. Our experience teaching thousands of leaders has shown us that digital marketing can be built upon two foundational models—the "1-9-90 Model" and the "5 Fundamentals of Digital Media Model." We will focus on these two models as we explore digital marketing in this chapter.

The 1-9-90 marketing model helps you see how your audience is creating content, sharing it, and accessing your story. The 5 Fundamentals of Digital Media model serves as a strategic filter to help ensure that your audience actually hears your story. The two are inextricable.

The 1-9-90 Model

Legendary department store merchant John Wanamaker once said: "Half of the money I spend on advertising is wasted. The trouble is I don't know which half." Well, we're getting closer every day to knowing the answer.

Regardless of the language they speak or the country in which they reside, we've seen a consistent trend across social media audiences: Less than 1% of a market creates new content; approximately 9% shares that content; and the other 90% lurks and learns, benefitting from the work of the creators and sharers. We've seen this model work in business-to-business and business-to-consumer markets throughout the world with remarkable consistency. We never see more than 1% of a market create content. On occasion, we'll see a larger share, up to 20%, of a market share content, but the proportion usually sticks pretty close to the 9% rule of thumb. The rest of us, always the overwhelming majority, are along for the ride.

The 1%

All three of these groups contain influencers. However, since the 1% are content creators, the number of influencers who really matter for your topic, brand, or country is relatively small. In fact, in all our work, we have never seen a case where more than 50 people were driving the majority share of content and influence for a market. And these influencers shape our conversations more than we realize. They might be driving the story you care about, the story of the larger category, or perhaps even the story for your competitor. The first question to ask yourself is: "Who are they?"

The diversity of influencers has become increasingly relevant for brands. They vary by country, language, topic, and subtopic—even for the same brand. This occurs because all content-creating influencers are passionate about a particular topic or set of topics, and they go deep on them. They don't care about everything you care about. Their range is different. And once you identify them, you can build a modern-day outreach list of exactly who matters and match it up against your brand message. This is your new media list.

The 9%

The next group is akin to community organizers. They like to share content to inform their audience. It is our job to ensure they have the content they desire so they can lead the way in sharing our story. If you are intent on getting your message out and then amping it up with a constant cycle of more advertising and more content, you'll discover over time how ineffective this approach is. We have to let our audience tell our story with us. We can't just tell it ourselves and think it will gain traction.

The 9% thrives on the recognition and respect of the audiences they serve. In fact, many of the 9% don't consciously realize their role. They're just doing their thing. They are active online, sharing, signing up, downloading, commenting and taking other actions that let their communities and peers know how they feel about certain topics. As such, the 9% serves as your "trust filter" for the market. They help define your authenticity and signal the audiences you care about whether you're worth listening to. You don't really need a trust ranking from an accredited institution anymore. You have one right in front of you. Is your audience sharing, commenting, and adding to your story? And are they reaching the communities you care about?

The 90%

This brings us to the 90% who lurk and learn. They typically come in contact with your story via search and social media channels, ranging from Twitter to LinkedIn to Facebook. Many of us confuse passivity in sharing content with having a passive attitude toward it. On the contrary, many people place a high degree of trust in the 1% and 9% and look to them to decide if they will make certain decisions.

Executing on the 1-9-90 Model

Now, let's imagine you are getting ready to promote a new story of importance to your organization. Take these key steps first:

1. **Define your story**: How many topics or subtopics are important to this story?

2. **Estimate the 1%**: Who are the influencers who most frequently write on these topics (e.g., journalists, bloggers, forum participants, or YouTube video creators)?

3. **Identify the 9%**: Who normally shares, likes, or comments on these topics, and how many of this group might be part of your 9%? Look at your Twitter accounts or those of like-minded organizations and see who is active.

4. **Analyze the 90%**: Write down the top queries one could make to learn more about your story in search. Go to the first page of each query and write down which people or outlets or organizations show up. From here, you can see which of the 1% and 9% are influencing the 90%. You might want to place even more emphasis on getting to know the members of this group. If you can access media algorithms, you can get complete precision in doing this. If you have zero budget, you can still take these steps on your own.

5. **Follow the influencers**: Go through all the social media channels where your key influencers and sharers actively participate and follow them there. In doing so, you take a step toward acting like your own media outlet, and you can make it easier for the people who care most about your story to access and share it.

If you stay focused on the 1-9-90 model, it will become an obsession. You will realize that you can discover exactly who cares about your story, who shapes the marketplace, and how you can improve search engine optimization and drive down your search engine marketing costs. You will also start to see that a new form of media planning is right around the corner, since your work will recalibrate the media outlets that actually matter. And, just as quickly, you will see the ones that don't.

5 Fundamentals of Digital Media Model

Anyone with any marketing in their background will probably recall the 4P's Model—price, product, place and promotion. In place for decades, it remains highly relevant and is a sister to the newer 5 Fundamentals of Digital Media Model. This new digital media model focuses on these five fundamentals:

1. **Insights:** Do you have insights that you can act on right now?

2. **Influencers:** Do you know who shapes your story, in priority order, for the 1%, the 9% and the 90%?

3. **Language:** Do you know the top 15 keywords and phrases that drive people to your story?

4. **Content**: Do you know the specific content that your audience desires?

5. **Channel**: Do you know where to reach each segment of your audience with the right content from the right people at the right time?

When we talk with the leaders of various organizations and brands, we find that none of them do all five at a high level. None of them, so don't feel bad as a newbie to this approach. Think of this as an aspirational strategic filter.

Insights

The number of PowerPoint slide decks, metrics, coverage reports, and other tools to tell us what might have happened between our communications and the marketplace are overwhelming—and often largely irrelevant. What truly matters is more powerful, yet far harder to discover. We want to find the *insights* that are actionable. If an insight leads to an idea and a way to reshape our environment, we are making progress. If an "insight" is merely good to know, it is little more than just a data point. You should probably terminate most of the reports you receive and rethink what you are measuring and why. If you are tough on yourself, you will travel the road to actionable insights. And you will streamline your time and probably save some resources.

Influencers

In the spirit of the 1-9-90 Model, think of our online world as a human media network. Which humans matter when trying to reach everyone else? How many types of influencers matter to you by topic, subtopic, or language? An important aspect of this also revolves around who influences the influencer. In general, the answer is four or fewer people. We call that small subset "subject-matter experts" (SMEs). They're usually not well known, but they are highly respected for their expertise in their relatively narrow field. They might know privacy rules inside and out, or be an expert on human rights in Africa. Content creators find them, as should you. They would love to hear from you.

Language

Humans always follow patterns in life and online. We like to think we are unique, but we tend to herd. When people search for topics or stories, they often use a similar set of words or phrases. As a result, we can use Google Search Analytics to determine the top 15 keywords or phrases that are most often used by the audiences we care about. Once we define those keywords or phrases, we have a number of possibilities for putting them to work. We might use them in website content and tag all our external content with them (e.g. videos, news releases, posts, etc.). We can use the same words within that same external content itself, and then ensure any related channels or sites pick up that content to amplify the effect. The rationale is clear: We are helping our audience find our story by using the right language. We are improving the alignment between our organization and our customers or citizens.

Content

Now we focus on content. We know what the marketplace desires (insights), we know who is telling or sharing our story (influencers) and we know the language they're using. If we look more closely at this audience, we can also see what content they desire. Fairly straightforward analysis will reveal the topics they most often talk about, the style of content they prefer, their preferred length for that content, and what irritates them and why. By closely scrutinizing our audience, the answers to these questions become even clearer over time. This knowledge can impact how you build your editorial plan for your organization, it can change how you organize content on your website, it can determine the content you emphasize on your social channels, and it shows where you might have a great message but have yet to persuade your audience to care about it as much as you do. Ultimately, you can see how to increase the alignment of your story with the audience you care about.

Channel

This is really the modern-day "placement" from the 4P's model, as applied to digital media. Placement in this case refers to channels, which range from social media platforms to search engines to external websites to your own website. The good news is that when you study your audience, you will once again see that audiences follow patterns. They tend to use no more than four channels to learn about a story. The key is that those four channels may be rather wide—for instance, Facebook, Twitter, Google, and key mainstream media publications. Once you know this pattern, you can get creative in how you reach your audience. You might post more tweets if you want to influence your search position on Google. You might feature Facebook posts that link back to your website so people can learn more about a story. You could feature YouTube videos on Twitter to introduce your audience to new channels. Or you might share key media stories from their favorite outlets on your social media channels. Once you know what your audience likes and where they hang out to learn, find ways to promote your message across all those channels.

Work hard, get smart

Both the 1-9-90 model and the 5 Fundamentals of Digital Media model are intended to help us better understand who shapes our story or who could, so we can better align with our audience. They require effort, but your knowledge is cumulative. You will be able to build your media model over time and use this information in increasingly sophisticated ways. However, if you don't invest in the hard work these two models require, you'll have a different experience. You'll hire consultants or do it yourself, do whatever feels right in the moment, and then realize you don't know how to scale your efforts.

As an added benefit, focusing on these models will help you stay on the right side of the law, particularly when it comes to data and privacy issues. These policy concerns, which you hear frequently discussed these days, can sound abstract and even a bit scary. For example, where should you store your data or how do you maintain privacy of information? If you know how your media model works, how you access your information, and what you plan to do to reach your audience, it becomes much easier to know how to stay within the laws of the land in these areas. Our experience is that you can still be quite creative and impactful while respecting regulations anywhere in the world. But you have to build the expertise in what you are doing to understand where the bright lines are and where the gray areas begin.

Sir Winston Churchill uttered the quote that starts this chapter in the House of Commons on October 28, 1944: "We shape our dwellings, and afterwards our dwellings shape us." He was making the point that an architect designs a building, but over time those who work or live inside the building redefine it. We are all architects of our story. If we shape our messages and align with our audience, the people who live inside our story will redefine it and create opportunities that we could never have imagined alone.

Great models unlock performance that doesn't require more work. Instead, they run so efficiently and smartly that the marketplace willingly takes over much of the heavy lifting. The two great models discussed in this chapter are a starting point. Can you do more in the future? Of course, but you need to start with the basics and get those right first. You can't expect to hit 300-yard drives down the middle of the fairway the first time you pick up a golf club. Start instead with the right grip and the right stance. That's what these two models can do for your marketing game.

Social Media —
The Opportunities and Challenges Ahead

Gary Briggs
Former Chief Marketing Officer at Facebook

Managing a brand, more than ever, means managing the conversations about your business. Those conversations predominantly happen in two places today—among friends in the "offline world" and online through social media.

The tools to manage your brand online and get insight into the conversations about it continue to improve. You need to be able to glean insight from major platforms, such as Facebook, Twitter, and Instagram, as well as Reddit and messaging platforms. You are limited to public-facing pages (i.e., not private pages or encrypted networks), so it's helpful to work with the influencers who attract users to their private pages and can help manage your message.

As with any messaging, you need to ensure that the more consumers learn about your brand, the more you live up to their expectations for transparency. You need to work with influencers and partners who are who they say they are, and who are forthright with their followers.

Overcome these three social media challenges to grow:

- **Organization:** You have to have strong data analysts on your team in addition to strong creative, media, and brand resources. The modern marketing leader needs to have great math skills as well as creative skills. If you don't have that personally, then hire for your weaknesses.

- **Speed:** The best online and social marketers generate new creative in hours, not days or weeks. You have to build an organization around you that creates faster than your competitors.

- **Insight:** If you build a modern organization and operate at speed, you then need to test, learn, and adapt. It's true that data win arguments. You can't predict what creative will perform better, but with today's tools to analyze and adjust your creative on the fly, you don't have to anymore.

Stay focused on your target, as always, and create conversations that operate in real time to build your brand and business. ▪

CHAPTER 11

Issues Management

> **"The problem with quotes on the Internet
> is that it is hard to verify their authenticity."**
> –Abraham Lincoln (source: The Internet)

If we were on a sailboat together for an afternoon, we would probably comment on the great weather, the size of the waves, or the design of the boat. Most of our world for those few hours would revolve around what was in plain sight.

Those in the spheres of business and government, unfortunately, often look at the world in a similar fashion. We react to what others are discussing in the press, we note what we hear at an all-hands meeting, or we reflect on life in the cafeteria. We respond to the environment we live in. We are less responsive or perhaps oblivious to issues that could make a difference for our brand in the near future.

During that sailing trip, a lot goes on beneath the surface. Fish swim by in schools, currents move at their own pace 60 feet below the surface, and the menaces of the deep exist outside our awareness. Yet, as marketers tasked with persuading people to embrace our desired behavior, we need to constantly be on the lookout for messages that jeopardize our goals.

Kip is on the board of 5.11 Tactical, the world's largest tactical clothing and equipment company and a leading supplier for the U.S. military and police departments across the country. The motto at 5.11 is "Always Be Ready"—it's an appropriate mantra when it comes to managing issues that threaten our businesses and lives, too.

Three keys to issues management

Issues management is only possible if we work to understand what is happening beneath the surface, so to speak. In handling difficult issues with activist groups such as PETA or Greenpeace; terrorist incidents from anthrax to bombings; or simply individuals upset with the status quo, we've developed three key insights worth sharing.

1. **Show your adversary respect**: Even though you might not like your adversary and have every reason to believe they're up to no good, imagine they are well-intentioned, smart, and working with the same intensity you are as you apply the ABCDE communication model. If you think without emotion, you can start to map out how and why your adversary is taking or will take specific actions. Bob has been involved in two companies that were targeted by Greenpeace. In each case, he came away with a healthy respect for the passion and commitment of the organization's members, even if he didn't always agree with them.

2. **Understand your adversary's vision and priorities**: If you are war-gaming in your organization to outthink a competitor, you need to imagine how they will hit the market, what themes they will use, how many resources they have, and much more. Do the same when it comes to issues management. If Greenpeace doesn't like what you are up to, how does your issue rank in their world? As an example, Greenpeace might focus on 25 issues worldwide and your issue—let's say it is palm oil (which the organization opposes when used in products sourced from companies that it deems to be destroying rainforests)—might be their 20th priority. It's not nearly as important to them as nuclear energy, for example. Knowing that can make a big difference in the amount of time and

effort you put against this issue as compared with other issues you have to manage.

3. **Understand your adversary's patterns:** Human beings follow patterns, so naturally your antagonists also follow patterns. (Turns out they are human, too.) This means we can see which social media channels they prefer, how they normally start a "fight," which spokespeople they use, how long they typically target an organization, and what they appear to view as success.

So how do we derive these three key insights? Where can we get the necessary information to make decisions to protect or promote our brand or organization? It turns out that the answers are right in front of us.

How to do your homework

An adversary rarely takes an organization completely by surprise. Make a list of the main touch points your customers or members have with your organization. Now, look backward for connections between them and the group that wrote letters or emails to you, called your help lines, complained about you in external community forums, railed on topics on your social media sites. When your adversaries have made those connections, they have done so for a reason. They want to see how awake you are and how easy a target you might be to achieve their goal, whatever that is. In business, you love competitors who are half-asleep—so do your competitors and antagonists.

As you do your research, you might find that your company receives 10,000 calls each year, and, within that group, 10 people consistently call to make statements rather than ask for help. You will always find complaints on your community forums, but a few people come to make statements rather than noting specific individual problems. And you might assume that complaints on social media sites are one-offs, but if you look for specific types of statements there, you often find a handful of people posting the same thing. These patterns often signal the work of adversaries, so note the names and their approach.

We can now discover the growing coalition of people who are working against our interests. We can't yet see if they are part of a larger group or if they are part of a spontaneous group starting to form. However, once we examine their language and patterns, we see that they use common statements and messaging, so we can conclude that they are part of the same group. We identify the members of the group and start tracking any mention they make about our organization, our products or services, or anyone else in our category. Sure enough, a month after our inventory, we see an uptick in conversation. It appears they are planning a larger action against our organization. Following the trail of evidence has led to a conclusion, and the conclusion has led to better intelligence and preparation.

This is just one general example we use to show why antagonist groups need to be discussed and, when appropriate, tracked daily to see the topics they care about and why. It is not unlike the way you would track normal, positive news about your company or organization. Too often, though, we get wrapped up in our own environment and focus exclusively on the positive. Did our customer satisfaction climb one point versus last quarter, and why? Did our social media likes on Facebook increase 10%, and why? How great are we and how many PowerPoint slides can we dedicate to this review of greatness? We tend to seek out positives to justify our expenditure of resources, rather than digging deep to figure out what problems might be lurking.

When Bob worked at Dell years ago, he put this theory into practice. Plenty of PowerPoint slide decks hit the screen with green-, yellow- and red-lighted activities, but none of them had the level of detail that would lead to insights on the actions they needed to take. His team looked into the forums, social media sites, and incoming complaints. Sure enough, the issues of paramount importance became clear, revealing the people who drove the negative attention and pointing toward the best responsive action to take. In his last year at Dell, his team began to identify issues in their earliest stages and could resolve them before they generated enough interest to gain widespread attention.

Issues management can be preventive, and it can save you money and time when done well. The size of your budget doesn't determine your approach or success. That comes from a desire to find the truth and address it.

What's your risk?

Too often, an organization defines a problematic issue as one that would make us uncomfortable if it hit the mainstream or trade press. Although this is important to consider since customers read the news, it is a very shallow view of issues management. From a big-picture perspective, you need to consider three more-encompassing facets of issues management. Organizations tend to be decent on the first, marginal at best on the second, and way behind on the third.

- **Reputational risk**: Will your CEO be singled out by a group? Will a group publicly state that you are polluting the environment or increasing cancer risk, or make another claim that could temporarily injure the reputation of the organization?

- **Financial risk**: It has never been easier to sell goods or services illicitly. In 2008, the Organization for Economic Cooperation and Development (OECD) estimated that the global counterfeit industry was about $200 billion. In 2016, with the advance of technology, the OECD speculated that the figure had grown to $461 billion. If you make a product or service that can be copied and the margin is high enough, then you are exposed to counterfeiting, whether you are aware of it or not. How many of the products or services from your organization or from the overall category are being diverted, and how many of your potential customers are receiving fake or black market product or services?

- **Disinformation risk**: How can others use fake content and new technologies to disrupt your organization or even you personally? Right now, we just talk about fake news. In the future, an antagonist will be able to create "deep fake" content that you never said but appears otherwise on manipulated videos or other compelling media. It might make it harder for you to enter a new market or to clarify a position on an important topic, so you need to stay on top of what is coming next, too.

Reputational risk

Companies typically face a similar set of chronic issues. To analyze and prepare for potential reputational risk, it helps to tick through the top chronic threats most companies need to deal with. These might change on the margin, and they might vary for non-commercial organizations, but most organizations will encounter many of these factors:

- Trademark and intellectual property disputes
- Product litigation
- Product crises (e.g., product recalls, software bugs, etc.)
- Environmental/advocacy crises
- Advertising deemed offensive
- Shareholder concerns
- Rogue employee/leaked confidential information
- Rumors
- Negative customer experience

To prepare for these potential threats, you need to sit down and go through each category so you can map out the issues you have today and anticipate the issues that might arise in the future. You then create a profile set of online keywords you can use to track these issues on social media platforms. With this, you will begin to see which topics are being mentioned in social media and whether they're the start of a major issue or an echo chamber for mainstream media. Either way, you'll start to see the world through a different lens.

The other way to prepare for crises relates to what we'll be asked while in the middle of one. Based on the work of Vincent T. Covello, founder of the Center for Risk Communication, we know there are 77 questions that people ask us over and over. (⬇ Online Exhibit 11.1) If we break down those questions further, it goes back to the 5Ws and 1H we learned in grade school—who, what, where, why, when, and how. Consumers, journalists, or the public at large ask these questions to ascertain what happened, what caused it to happen, and what does it mean.

Experts often trot out a separate model just for issues management. However, that isn't necessary if you follow the ABCDE Model, which works equally well for positive and negative issues. If you think about who your *audience* is for a negative issue, you often find it is much smaller than you first expect. Most of your customers rarely care about the issues that are making you sweat. Next, you focus on the *behavior* desired for the market, which might be as simple as an awareness of your response to the issue. You add in what your own organizational behavior will be to ensure it matches up with what you say—you walk the talk. When it comes to *content*, don't overdo it. You don't need ten pages of Q&A, for example; you need the one to three messages you want to disseminate to your audience. Regarding *distribution* and *execution,* you align it with whom you need to reach and how you'll judge success.

The key with issues of reputational risk is to avoid overcompensating. Just because you think something is an issue does not mean your audience does. Take the time to think it through, using the ABCDE Model.

Financial risk

We are entering a new chapter in issues management that directly impacts our bottom lines. If you make a product or service in, say, the healthcare, beauty, fashion, or automotive industries, someone is selling counterfeit goods that mimic your wares. It is remarkably easy to create new labels, fake medicine, consumer electronics, jewelry, handbags, and so on. If you are in retail, fake coupons are being made for what you sell. If you are in e-commerce, someone is creating fake reviews. If you are buying media, you might be buying an audience that is 25 % smaller than the numbers you have because they were inflated by bot networks.

To get a sense for the ease with which someone can carry out these illicit activities, let's imagine a small group of bad guys who want to create a bot network designed to sell counterfeit goods that undercut the product you sell to millions of loyal customers. If these bad actors were looking to make a killing on counterfeit medicines, here's how they might carry out their scheme:

- They create five to 10 fake personas for Twitter. Each one uses stock photos and bios that show a range of accomplishments.

- They visit their favorite site on the dark web and purchase followers, so each persona now has 100,000 to 200,000 followers.

- They automate key words for these fake personas to tweet—let's say it's about drugs for Parkinson's disease—and, at the same time, they create more fake personas with 5,000 to 10,000 followers, all of which retweet the earlier tweets.

- They let loose with other bots that retweet those tweets. In each, most of the keywords they use link to other websites.

- The search engines treat this retweeting as engagement and move their content up to the first screens for queries about drugs to treat Parkinson's.

- Now, unsuspecting citizens are searching for "Parkinson's disease, drugs, cheap," and seeing their illicit site ranked as higher or higher than your legitimate site.

- Their site appears to be a pharmacy based in Canada, but it doesn't really exist there, of course. Instead, the site links to a company in a faraway country, from which a fake version of the Parkinson's drug is now being shipped direct to customers via a special mailing system.

Even a slacker could build this whole model in a week or so. Changing it up to endlessly evade authorities is just as easy. It's the same system, by the way, that traffickers use to move contraband such as fentanyl and heroin. So, if we get good at stopping bad actors targeting our organizations, we might also indirectly help the entire world in battling the opioid epidemic.

This is far easier to combat for an organization with deep pockets, but it doesn't take a wealth of resources to effectively counter these risks. To do so, write down the top 100 search queries a person would make to find your product or service. Then go on Google or Bing and search those queries. What do you find? Anything strike you as odd? Counterfeiters and bad actors won't call you up, they won't write you letters, they don't complain in forums. They are counting on your being asleep at the wheel. Just doing this one simple exercise to see if you know every provider selling your goods or services, or those of your competitors, can reveal most of the bad actors trying to feed off your offering or your message. Then you can move to counter them and shore up your preventative measures. (See Box 11.1) Even if you are in the clear—or think you are—be sure to survey the category as a whole. If money can be made, bad actors will simply repeat their model endlessly until it stops working. So, remember ABR: *Always Be Ready*.

Building a Great Defense: Some Measures to Help Manage Risks

Lock up URLs and subdomains: Identify the available uniform resource locators (URLs) and the top 100 subdomains for the widest range of social channels you can imagine for your brand and campaigns. Then, lock them up. This will help you combat spammers, who routinely buy sites and create subdomains to steal traffic that should go to your site.

Build a central repository of passwords and IDs: Create a repository for the passwords and user IDs for every website and every social channel for every country in which you do business. Going country by country, do a sweep of all your brands' websites and social channels, deleting those you don't need. And ensure that all these sites and channels—including those of your agencies and contractors—are managed to the security standards of your IT department. Always look for the weakest links.

Do the top 100 queries exercise: What are the top 100 search queries about your brand? See anything unusual? What does it tell you?

War-game your antagonists: Study the habits of all your antagonists, just as you would your competitors. Show them respect in your planning.

Analyze your own language: Figure out the words and phrases that set off antagonists and simply stop using them, if you can.

Build specialized alert systems: Track your top ten chronic issues and top antagonist groups to learn what matters in the real world on a daily basis. Treat this news with the same respect you give your positive news.

Light a bonfire: Take your old standby statements and binders and enjoy the warmth of a good fire as you start planning how to manage risk and issues in new ways.

Disinformation

Disinformation includes activities or actions taken by a third party to share fake information to persuade or disrupt an audience. Given that new technologies make disinformation easier to disseminate and more effective upon arrival, it's an area well worth your time to study, understand, and anticipate what could arise in the future.

Perspective is key for understanding disinformation. In actuality, it's an old tactic that is evolving due to new technology and, in a few cases, massive support from various governments. The sponsor of disinformation might be a country already engaging in cyberwarfare with us, or it could be an organization inside that country whose values don't match our own. Here are a few examples:

- **Disrupting society**: Elections easily illustrate this point. In the United States, many people still wonder how much Russia tried to interfere with our 2016 presidential election. If we look at those who engage in disinformation, which certainly includes Russia, they follow patterns. And if you look closely at the *modus operandi* of Russia and its allies, there are dozens of examples of how that bloc has disrupted elections in country after country. It's not a question of whether they're doing it, but how they're doing it. In the future, organizational leaders will ask their teams: "How is disinformation being used to impact our business?" And they will need to get a real answer.

- **Entering a new country**: Disinformation could persuade the citizens of a country that your organization should not be part of their ecosystem. You might not realize that, long before you even thought of entering the country, someone had engaged in a multi-year effort to dissuade its citizens away from your organization or offering.

- **Intellectual property:** You believe you have patent protection, but the citizens of certain countries hear that you stole your IP directly from their country. Most of them don't mind if their homegrown organizations take it back.

- **Trade**: You believe you are going to work out a trade agreement with a given country or bloc of countries, but their citizens are hearing about how many jobs they will lose or how you don't care about their welfare.

What content do citizens consume in the countries you want to enter? How do they normally receive that content? In understanding how media works in Pakistan versus Germany versus Mexico versus the Ukraine, we start to see which media matter and how we might tell our story to decrease the chances that bias can lead to hate. Right now, we think of the counter-disinformation effort mainly as it applies to governments and extremist groups such as ISIS. In the future, if I am a bad actor and I want to ensure that a company or organization will have trouble expanding, I'm going to start reaching out to people the minute they can use a mobile phone. We all know how good Disney is at shaping brands at the earliest age possible. Disinformation experts think along the same lines. They are the Bizarro World counterpart to Disney, and they do their best to reach youth with their distorted views as soon as possible.

A new form of war

It has never been easier for bad actors to tamper with your organization's content. Digital technologies have opened all kinds of avenues for interference and disruption. There's a new form of war, raging ceaselessly online. Here are just a few examples of what bad actors can do to sabotage your organization:

- **The manufactured statement:** If you speak at a conference, you can download what you are saying in real time and have it automatically transcribed in the cloud. If a third party decides to change two points in your talk, he or she can use audio compression to remix your audio in the cloud, so it sounds exactly like you were making those two points, even if you were not. Voila! The manipulated transcript and audio go out for public consumption. Video and images can be manipulated just as easily.

- **A subtler version of fake news**: Using natural language processing, bad actors can create a summary of content about a topic within seconds. They then drop a new key message into the summary and send it out as news. Maybe 95 % of the news is now accurate, but it contains a totally false point.

- **Fully fake personas:** Pushing the false Twitter personas agenda further, imagine hundreds of fake personas entering a forum and fueling a very negative discussion. What no one realizes at the time is that the conversation is actually being conducted between bots that are designed to argue with one another. Manipulators can easily create credibility for fake personas, stage a fake debate between them, and potentially persuade and divide actual people.

You must prepare

The best way to solve crises is to prepare for them, and you should start your issues management preparation with a cold hard look at reputational risk. If you focus on constant, ongoing protection of your brand's and organization's reputational risk, you will start to see how you can elevate your approach over time to include financial risk and disinformation, as well. Equally important, you will become increasingly fluent in these topics, so you can discuss these risks with the Chamber of Commerce or other organizations who can help look out for the greater good of an industry or group of organizations.

For organizations of all stripes and in all parts of the world, issues management will only increase in value going forward. Our respect for an organization pursuing a cause will increase as it learns how to build the right approaches and relationships. Our trust in its mission will expand as it effectively counters opposing views in a civil manner. We all must remain vigilant against those who aim to disrupt our world.

How Diplomats Persuade Hostile Audiences

Teeta Manson
Acting Director and Public Affairs Officer, Bureau of Conflict and Stabilization
Operations, U.S. Department of State

While the U.S. has allies around the world, American diplomats often face hostile audiences—from the very real dangers of war zones, to tightly controlled foreign media, to a population opposed to the U.S. foreign policy position in their country. Here are some ways these diplomats get their messages across to challenging audiences to reach and persuade them:

1. Experiment with the tone and style of their message: Formal, well thought-out op-eds once led the way stylistically for how the U.S. government put forth messages overseas. Today, that is often distilled down to a Tweet. Embassies have become more creative as they have expanded beyond talking to counterparts in Ministries of Foreign Affairs. Now, they engage regularly with audiences ranging from at-risk youth, to religious leaders, and to women's groups. With greater diversity in audience came a need to diversify the tone and style of messages. In some of the most closed media environments, embassies have had success utilizing non-traditional techniques from cartoons to Periscope. These alternative styles and platforms have expanded their reach beyond traditional interlocutors.

   Bottom Line—Your message may be serious, but don't hesitate to experiment and adapt your tone and style to suit your audience. If your message doesn't connect or resonate with your audience, it won't be persuasive.

2. Be innovative in how you deliver your message: In some countries, U.S. government access to the media is still limited. Think of environments like China, Venezuela, or Syria. As a result, a few embassies have been reaching their audiences using SMS messages. In many countries, you can purchase numbers from phone providers based on addresses and other factors. It might feel old school compared to the latest options, such as Steemit and Vero, but SMS offers a way to deliver messages to a targeted group. All the receivers need is a cell phone signal. That makes it ideal for getting messages out to locations with limited internet access or where data costs for smart phones are beyond the reach of your primary audience. It is perfect for reaching remote villages, where

the only other news sources are tightly controlled foreign radio stations and TV channels.

Bottom Line—Staying current with the latest tech for reaching your audience is essential, but don't forget about the less flashy options if you work in a tough or heavily controlled media environment. The best message in the world isn't successful if it can't reach your target audience.

3. Be creative with who delivers your message: Gone are the days when foreign policy could only be delivered by ambassadors and press attachés. Today, U.S. embassies utilize everyone from newly minted diplomats to partnering organizations to communicate with the public. In more challenging locations, embassies have had success partnering with local organizations. And many embassies have had success with "Youth Ambassador" and "Celebrity Ambassador" messaging campaigns supporting everything from the environment to anti-drug messages. In some situations, your spokesperson won't be the most persuasive person to deliver your message. Always ask: Who will be more persuasive to your target audience—a stranger or someone your audience can identify with? Imagine asking your kid to clean their room, and then imagine your kid's friend coming over and mentioning something about the mess. Threats of grounding aside, who is more persuasive?

Bottom Line—Don't be afraid to empower others. Pick the person who is going to be the most persuasive to your audience and prepare them to deliver your message. ■

CHAPTER 12

Case Studies— From Startups to Fortune 500 Companies

"It's not creative unless it sells."
–David Ogilvy

W hen you were in school, it's a pretty good bet you would ask your teachers, your parents and often yourself, "When am I going to actually use this?" It's a fair question to ask about the ABCDE Model as well. Based on our work with hundreds of clients and diplomats from around the world, we know that you can use this model to tackle virtually any communication problem you're dealing with right now—whether it's figuring out how to turn around a failing business, get a neighborhood project underway, or help raise money for a worthy cause.

Let's get to work!

Theory is fine, but "real world" examples bring it to life. This chapter will show you how others have used the ABCDE Model to help their businesses. Even if you're not directly involved in running a company, you likely have a role in business as an employee, a retiree, a shareholder, or a customer. The better these businesses communicate their key messages to their target audiences in a compelling manner, the better it is for all of us.

The core problem most businesses have today—especially struggling firms—is that they do not offer their customers a meaningful difference when compared with their competition. Instead of trying to create something special that appeals to the target audience, they rely on short-term incentives or marketing gimmicks to get consumers to pick them. This can lead them to make promises they can't keep, which creates customer churn and results in a lack of brand loyalty. The ABCDE Model is not designed to fix a "bad" product or the lack of a differentiated product. Nor is it intended to be a "how to" guide for creating a new business. Those are huge challenges worthy of a whole library of books (which already exist). But if you are going to create a new product or service, or you are trying to figure out how to position your existing products or services, the ABCDE Model can be a helpful tool for evaluating whether you have a compelling message when you're ready to go to market.

Many entrepreneurs get so excited about their new product they think it will sell itself. Bad news: It won't. While P&G spends more than $7 billion a year globally on various forms of advertising, it also spends a whopping $2 billion on research and development. They spend all that money to ensure that, when their consumers have their "moments of truth" with a P&G product—when they pick it up off the shelf or when they use it—the product delivers what the advertising promised. In other words, the *reason to believe* is engineered directly into the product design before the first case ships. Promises made; promises kept.

Rather than relying on deep price discounting or marketing gimmicks, smart businesses take the time to understand who their target audience is and what they really want and need. They focus on delivering a meaningful benefit and crafting messages that give those prospective buyers a credible reason to believe the brand can deliver that benefit consistently over time. And then they deliver on that benefit. This is the only way to stand out from the competition in the long run.

What "Mad Men" were mad about

Back in the heyday of television advertising (from the early 1960s through the late 1980s), there was a raging debate between advertising agencies whose executives believed in the value of "image" or "thematic" ads versus those that emphasized something superior about the product. These advertising claims were often in the form of a slogan—the M&M's candy "melts in your mouth, not in your hand" line, for example.

The work of Rosser Reeves, one of the original "Mad Men," is portrayed in the well-known AMC television series. He was the creator of what he called the "USP," or unique selling proposition. According to Reeves, the primary goal of any advertising should be to sell something. (His archrival, David Ogilvy, believed the same thing.) Reeves was convinced that only by hammering home your product's USP, ideally with a catchy turn of phrase, would you be successful in the marketplace.

For those of us who have spent our careers in marketing and advertising, this isn't an "either/or" debate. You need both a USP (i.e., key benefit), as well as a brand persona. For example, while it's true that Apple makes terrific products, how you *feel* about Apple is just as, or perhaps even more, important. When you decide to buy a brand, you're not just making a product decision. You're making a statement about what's important to you and what you want to be publicly associated with.

With this historical context in mind, let's turn our attention to some examples of how companies use the ABCDE Model to build their business and improve their communications. The first case study is a business that, as we wrote this in mid-2019, was just getting underway. The beauty of the ABCDE Model is it can guide anyone who wants to create a truly valuable brand that consumers will trust and interact with.

> *Each of the following case studies uses a grid to organize the ABCDE communication model and make it easier to share with others as well as to help you make sure you cover all the strategic questions. We have posted a downloadable version of this grid for you to use on our website www.craftingpersuasion. com. We encourage you to use it as well.*

Case study #1:
Turning a weakness into a strength

Ryan May is a world-class sailor. He's been hooked since he was eight and has sailed many seas and oceans around the world. He loves sailing so much he wants to make his living doing it. A year ago, with his father's help, he brought a small 24-foot sailboat from Canada to the San Francisco Bay and started offering charter boat rides. His boat can hold four customers comfortably—six if they are willing to squeeze in a bit.

Recently, when one of the authors asked him how business was going, he said he was operating at a loss. If business did not improve soon, he would have to consider giving it up. His wife was working full-time and was starting to question if Ryan was building a business or enjoying a hobby. The problem was competition; other sea captains offered sailing excursions on San Francisco Bay, one of the most beautiful and iconic waterways in the world. Most of Ryan's competitors had bigger boats, such as catamarans, which could take on a lot more passengers. Because of the smaller size of his boat, he was having a tough time attracting customers away from his larger competition.

Ryan wasn't offering a unique branded experience. He was offering a generic product in a crowded category that is pretty price sensitive. His competition had a natural advantage—they could take out more clients per trip, which generated more revenue and profits than he could hope for. So, we shared the ABCDE Model with him. While he thought it was interesting, he didn't see how it had anything to do with his business. After all, he was the captain of a ship, not a marketer. We urged him to go through the ABCDE Model to see if it could help save his business. First, we summarized the problem. How could he compete against the larger sailboats? How could he turn the smaller size of his boat into a competitive edge against the larger boats, and thus grow his revenue and profits?

We started the discussion by looking at "A" (Audience). He noted that his client size was limited to just four passengers per trip. He was charging $125 per person for a 3-hour tour, so if he got a full boat with four passengers—something that only occurred about half the days he offered excursions—he would generate $500 per trip. And since he typically only sailed once a day, that was his maximum daily revenue.

Unfortunately, on many days, he would get only two clients, or $250 per trip. Even worse, there were days in which no one signed up for a trip, the boat never left the dock, and he generated no revenue at all.

It matters how you define the problem

In thinking about how to create more demand for his sailing trips, Ryan was initially just trying to get more people to sign up by working with other companies, such as AirBnB, which offers its boarders experiences in the cities where they stay. He had to change his thinking about the problem and instead ask: "Who would be willing to pay a premium price for a sailing experience with just two customers? And why?" It was after we restated the business problem that we came up with a new idea that answered that question definitively—staging wedding proposals for couples.

The breakthrough idea was based on a key consumer insight: Most couples like to have a unique and special engagement memory. They want to have a story they can share with their friends and family (and eventually their children). Getting engaged in just any setting won't do. What could be more romantic than proposing to your future spouse, just the two of you sailing on San Francisco Bay with the sun slowly setting to the west?

Once we identified this right niche audience, the rest of the idea generation went quickly. The "B" (Behavioral Objective) was simple: persuade couples who wanted to get engaged to have their wedding proposal on Ryan's sailboat. Questions about "C" (Content) and the primary benefit, the reasons to believe, and the brand persona (i.e., tone and character) quickly had answers, too:

- **Benefit:** "Make this special moment memorable for a lifetime."

- **Reason to believe:** "We're the only ones who offer this unique experience to propose to your partner on an intimate sailboat with flowers, champagne, music, and a video of the entire event."

- **The tone and character:** "Fun, caring, and romantic."

We then discussed what "D" (Delivery) would entail. In addition to making some adjustments to the actual sailboat and sailing experience—such as outfitting the boat with speakers and cameras to play music and record the wedding proposal—there were several ways Ryan could deliver his content to this target audience. For example, he would need to create a new website totally focused on selling wedding proposal sailing trips. Ryan secured the perfect URL for his forthcoming website: www.proposalsonthebay.com.

He was planning to go to the next Bay Area Wedding Fair and team up and cross-promote with other businesses that cater to the wedding market, such as wedding planners, country clubs, travel agencies, and the like. He could get a marketing intern to handle all the digital marketing for this new business, including paid search, content marketing, and so on.

The final element of the model—the "E" (Evaluation)—would be easy to measure. How many trips could he book, and what kind of revenue could he generate? Pricing for the wedding proposal trips could range from $499 for a base package, all the way up to $999 for a premium package with chocolates, champagne, video and other perks. At those rates, Ryan could easily double his revenue in a year and increase his profits by an even wider margin, even if he only did one engagement sailing trip a day. There was a good chance he could be 100% booked by the end of his first year, maybe even have a waiting list, once the word got out to locals and out-of-town visitors in his target audience.

If the business succeeded as anticipated, Ryan could eventually branch out to other specialized events, such as wedding anniversaries and birthday celebrations, with other boats and dedicated websites. Ryan was excited about focusing his current business on a niche market with a unique offering that justified premium pricing. It would create a valuable "brand" to compete in a highly competitive market. What had been a liability—his smaller sailboat—had become a competitive advantage that would be hard to match.

FIGURE 12.1
The ABCDE Grid for ProposalsontheBay.com

Audience	Couples looking for a special engagement event
• Audience Insight	People want a romantic story about the day they got engaged that they can share with friends and family—and eventually their children.
Behavioral Objectives	Sign up on www.proposalsonthebay.com to go on a unique, private sailing trip on San Francisco Bay to propose to your loved one. It will be the memory of a lifetime (with flowers, chocolates, music and more).
Content	
• Benefit	Create a special memory for a lifetime when proposing to the person you want to marry.
• Reason to Believe	We take care of everything for proposing to your spouse-to-be during an intimate sailing trip. This includes a seasoned captain, flowers, music, champagne, and other accoutrements that will make this an experience you'll remember the rest of your life.
• Tone/Character	Fun, caring and romantic
Delivery—Media	Creative use of PR (such as ads and placed stories in the *San Francisco Chronicle*) and human-interest stories (such as local television stations air on occasions like Valentine's Day), social media (Twitter, Facebook, Instagram), strategic partnerships with other Bay Area companies in the bridal business, SEO and paid adwords (to drive website traffic).
Delivery—Message	"Propose to your spouse while sailing on San Francisco Bay!"

(continues on next page)

(Figure 12.1 continued)	
• On Brand	Focus on ProposalsontheBay.com brand name.
• Recognizable	High utilization of images of SF Bay as well as romantic sailing photos.
• Simple	Solely focus on marriage proposal occasion
• Attention Grabbing	Simple graphics and romantic imagery
Evaluation	Number of bookings and total revenue

This business had the potential to be highly differentiated from the competition. It could justify premium pricing and would have much better profit margins compared to the current business. If he were trying to raise money from outside investors for his current business versus the new wedding proposal business, the contest would not even be close.

Creating a premium brand in a specialized niche is much more likely to generate strong revenue and profits compared to a generic brand in a very competitive market. Ryan is hard at work getting ready to launch his new business. In future editions of this book we'll let you know just how well he did!

Case study #2:
Turning a generic product into a superstar

During childhood, many of our favorite breakfast memories are of eating pancakes with our family. In fact, table syrup is one of the most ubiquitous items you will find in U.S. pantries, with more than 80% of households having it on hand. What you might not know or appreciate is what most Americans think of as maple syrup (Aunt Jemima, for example) is anything but—it's high fructose corn syrup with a bunch of added artificial and natural ingredients.

Real maple syrup is a big business, and there's a good reason Canadians put the maple leaf on the national flag. Each year, Canada produces more than 12.5 million gallons of this "liquid gold" (which retails for $40 to $60 per gallon, compared to $8 for table syrup). One primary reason maple syrup is so expensive is that it takes 40 gallons of maple sap to make a single gallon of maple syrup.

Canadians dominate the category, with more than 70% of global production, the majority of which is consumed by Americans. The United States is a distant second in terms of maple syrup production, with just 4.2 million gallons a year. The iconic state of Vermont is responsible for most of the U.S. production, with more than 1.3 million gallons. New York is second, with about 500,000 gallons.

All these fun facts were worth noting if you were a marketing consultant who got a call in 2010 from Robb Turner (as one of our authors was). Robb was the owner of a successful energy hedge fund and had recently purchased 800 acres of land in upstate New York to relax on the weekends. The property came with more than 20,000 maple trees and, unfortunately, a huge annual property tax bill.

Robb asked if there was any way he could reduce his property tax, and he learned his only option was to use his land for agriculture. Given that the property hadn't been farmed since the Civil War, and he didn't want to chop down 20,000 beautiful maple trees to clear the land for crops, the only logical answer was to make maple syrup. So that's what he started to explore.

Robb, a West Point-trained engineer, decided to take advantage of those skills and figure out a better way to make maple syrup. He planned to make what would turn out to be one of the largest maple syrup production operations in the United States. Since he was in the energy business, he thought there might be some best practices he'd picked up along the way in extracting natural gas that he could apply to maple syrup production.

Turns out Robb was right. Using reverse osmosis to extract the excess liquid (rather than heating the sap to evaporate it, which is the traditional process) resulted in an incredibly pure product. He bought one of the biggest reverse-osmosis machines manufactured and installed it in a 27,000-square-foot "sugarhouse" on his property. His team utilized 400,000 taps to get the sap directly from the trees, many of them more than a century old. (⬇ Online Exhibit 12.1) The result is a process that is sustainable and consistent, and yields a fully organic product that's sweeter than the maple syrup that comes out of Canada or Vermont. In consumer taste tests, it had a noticeably richer and smoother taste than the competition. So, rather than blend his maple syrup with lower-quality syrups to increase his total output, Robb insisted on keeping his syrup all in the same batch—similar to what wineries do when they make single-batch origin wines.

Robb was confident he could make a superior maple syrup. After all, this is exactly the kind of challenge engineers love. But he knew he would need a premium brand as well as a robust marketing program if this was going to be worth the huge amount of time and financial investment required. From a marketing perspective, the good news was there weren't a lot of nationally known maple syrup brands. Before he got underway, Robb would ask friends and family if they could name a maple syrup brand. The answer was almost always no.

Robb wanted a brand name that communicated that this was going to be the premier brand in the maple syrup category. After considering several alternatives, we worked with him to select "Crown Maple." The name was a play on words with the crown of a tree, as well as an indication that this syrup was worthy of the most discriminating consumer. To make his maple syrup stand out on the shelf, we worked with Robb to settle on a different kind of bottle from traditional maple syrup (you know, the ones in the shape of a maple leaf). We decided to use scotch bottles, which showed off the beautiful golden maple syrup in a proprietary way. (⬇ Online Exhibit 12.2)

We then focused on using the ABCDE Model to create a marketing message that would motivate foodies to buy and try his new brand:

- **Audience:** To create an air of exclusivity, Robb hired the former sommelier at Per Se, one of the top restaurants in New York City, to be his lead salesperson. Using their various connections, we were able to get Crown Maple introduced as a branded ingredient in a number of leading restaurants, as well as in products such as chocolate bars, granola, and ice cream. By the time Crown Maple showed up in the local Dean & DeLuca's or Whole Foods, there was an audience familiar with the brand and already interested in buying it for home use. Consumers who didn't live close to a Costco or other retailer that carried Crown Maple could find it on Amazon.

- **Behavioral Objective:** This was simple enough—get enough consumers to buy Crown Maple to keep it in distribution across the United States. While getting a new product launched across the country is extremely challenging, Robb achieved national distribution and a healthy amount of online sales after an intense effort to create consumer excitement for the brand.

- **Content**: The benefit Crown Maple was promising was the taste and purity of organic maple syrup. The reason to believe was an integral part of how Robb envisioned making the product from the very beginning—a "closed system" in which the maple sap goes directly from the tree to the bottle. The tone and character of everything related to Crown Maple would be authentic, natural, and sophisticated.

- **Delivery:** We translated the copy strategy of taste, quality, and reason to believe with the selling line: "Quite possibly the purest maple syrup on Earth." We wanted to ensure this marketing message got delivered far and wide to the select target audience. We placed a steady stream of articles in publications, including the *New York Times* and various gourmet publications—the preferred media of his audience. The company hosted events at Madava Farms (the site of Crown Maple) to encourage families and foodies to experience the maple syrup and the environment first hand. We used social media extensively to celebrate Crown Maple throughout the year, especially when the sap was flowing and the syrup was being made.

- **Evaluation:** The primary metric Robb was looking at was sales volume. While the launch process has not been easy, the business is now profitable and continues to grow at a steady clip. What's been equally gratifying is the recognition Crown Maple has received. It won "Best of Show" at the 2015 Winter Fancy Food Show and has become what Robb envisioned when he first had an idea of what he could produce on his 800 acres of century-old maple trees—one of the leading premium maple syrup brands.

(For more information, check out www.crownmaple.com. We highly recommend buying the product as well to taste how truly amazing it is!)

FIGURE 12.2
The ABCDE Grid for Crown Maple

Audience	Foodies who want the very best in what they eat.
• Audience Insight	Consumers are willing to pay a premium price for a maple syrup if it has something unique to offer versus the competition (from Canada as well as the United States).
Behavioral Objectives	Purchase the entire line of Crown Maple products (for your home, in restaurants, and as an ingredient in other food products).
Content	
• Benefit	Enjoy the exceptional taste of the purest maple syrup.
• Reason to Believe	Reverse osmosis filters out all impurities between the maple tree and the processing unit. Crown Maple literally goes from the tree to the bottle in pristine condition.
• Tone/Character	Authentic, natural, sophisticated.
Delivery—Media	Heavy use of PR (such as the *New York Times*) and human interest stories (such as *Martha Stewart*), social media (Twitter, Facebook, Instagram), live events (at Fancy Food Show, at Madava Farms, etc.), SEO and paid adwords (to drive website traffic)
Delivery—Message	"Quite possibly the purest maple syrup on earth."
• On Brand	Everything associated with Crown Maple is always all natural and premium.
• Recognizable	Strong use of Crown Maple logo and distinctive bottle shape

• Simple	Emphasis on purity of product.
• Attention Grabbing	Utilize packaging and product quality to tell the story of Crown Maple's heritage and excellence.
Evaluation	Annual sales of Crown Maple (total and by channel); growth of e-commerce business.

Case study #3:
Who really loves to drive a Subaru?

In 1995, the executive team at Subaru was having a tough time. They had just released their first luxury car and hired a new ad agency to launch it—and sales bombed. The follow-up research they did indicated most drivers thought Subaru was a reliable but drab car—and certainly not one they would ever consider a luxury automobile.

So, rather than try to compete against the Big Four auto companies and continue to go after a mass market of car drivers, the company's marketing team decided to focus instead on key demographic segments who liked driving a Subaru. According to an article in the *Atlantic* magazine, their targets included "teachers and educators, health-care professionals, IT professionals, and outdoorsy types." While updating their marketing research, the Subaru team discovered a fifth group: lesbians. Marketing specialist Paul Poux, who set up their focus groups, learned lesbian Subaru owners "felt it fit them and wasn't too flashy."

The marketing team decided to go after all five consumer segments with focused advertising that would appeal to each user group. For health care professionals, they placed heavy emphasis on getting them to the hospital in any kind of weather. For outdoors types, Subaru's four-wheel drive and the ability to navigate dirt roads became primary points of emphasis. But advertising directed at lesbians in the mid-1990s was not going to be easy. The Clinton administration was pushing its "Don't Ask, Don't Tell" military policy and Congress passed the Defense of Marriage Act. Gay characters were still pretty rare in popular movies and television (Ellen came out in 1997), and the public backlash against the types of shows and commercials that supported a gay lifestyle could be swift and brutal.

Given the current state of their business, though, the Subaru marketing team decided to forge ahead. According to Ron Dicker, a reporter at the *Huffington Post*, getting buy-in from their Japanese management made for a somewhat funny story: "When one Subaru ad man…proposed the gay-targeting ads in talks with Japanese executives, the executives hurriedly looked up 'gay' in their dictionaries. Upon reading the definition, they nodded at the idea enthusiastically. Who wouldn't want happy or joyous advertising?" When the senior management finally understood what was being asked, approval came much faster than the U.S. team expected. Turns out that a similar ad campaign had run in Canada several years earlier and generated positive results.

The advertising agency decided they would utilize hidden messages in creating the ads. In an interview with AdRespect, the agency's creative director John Nash said: "We've found that playful coding is really, really appreciated by our consumers. They like deciphering it." So, one campaign included cars bearing various license plates that said P-TOWN, referring to Provincetown, Massachusetts, a popular LGBT vacation spot. The headlines often had double meanings—such as "Get Out. And Stay Out."—that could refer to driving a Subaru in the wild or coming out of the closet. Another headline—"It's not a choice. It's the way we're built."—boasted both the Subaru's quality and referenced the fact that being gay is innate. (⬇ Online Exhibit 12.3)

When the advertising launched in 1996, some consumers wrote the company to proclaim they would never buy a Subaru again. But once the marketing team discovered that none of the letter writers had ever purchased a Subaru in their life, the threat rang hollow. The U.S. ad campaign was a hit, and sales improved. Subaru was the first major company in the United States to launch an ad campaign that was openly supportive of the LGBT community. It showed they cared about their customers and the causes that were important to them. Subaru turned around a difficult business situation by taking the time to understand their target audience and finding a message that would resonate with them.

While we obviously don't have any internal Subaru documents, we think the strategy would look something like this (Figure 12.3):

FIGURE 12.3

The ABCDE Grid for Subaru's Ads Focused on Lesbian Customers

Audience	Lesbians interested in owning or leasing a reliable car.
• Audience Insight	Marketing research indicated lesbians in the United States were four times more likely to buy a Subaru compared to the average car buyer. This is because lesbians believed Subarus were well built and had many of the features they said they wanted in a vehicle (e.g., reliable, operated in all kinds of weather and road conditions).
Behavioral Objectives	Get more lesbian singles and lesbian couples to purchase a Subaru (and recommend buying one to their friends).
Content	
• Benefit	You'll love your Subaru because of the many ways it loves you.
• Reason to Believe	Subarus have four-wheel drive that enables them to handle all kinds of roads and conditions, plus they have plenty of room to carry whatever you want. We understand and connect with you more than any of the Big 4 auto companies.
• Tone/Character	Authentic, caring, playful.
Delivery—Media	Selective and targeted use of print, radio, outdoor and television advertising.
Delivery—Message	"It's not a choice. It's the way we're built."
• On Brand	Ads theme tied to rugged Subaru heritage. ("We are not like the Big 4. We are independent and proud of it.")

• Recognizable	Subaru product featured as hero of ads.
• Simple	Clever use of humor.
• Attention Grabbing	Hidden messages to gay customers to show Subaru's understanding of and empathy for target audience.
Evaluation	Sales of Subaru vehicles to lesbian owners.

Case study #4:
Reviving your grandfather's brand

If a brand is highly successful, it can outlive its creator—think Walt Disney, Steve Jobs at Apple, or Henry Ford. Of course, the vast majority of brands don't last for long periods of time. Hundreds of them come and go every year. Even enduring brands like Sears, which was an innovator in retail for well over a century, can ultimately die.

One of the rarest of all success stories in business is a brand that is on the ropes and comes roaring back to life. That's exactly the story of Old Spice, and it's helpful to look at its resurgence through the perspective of the ABCDE Model.

Old Spice products were first sold by William Lightfoot Schultz, who founded his business in 1934 as a soap and toiletries company aimed at women (just like a cigarette company called Marlboro). But given his lack of success with a female audience, he shifted over to selling Old Spice products for men in 1938. Schultz emphasized sailing ships on the packaging, featuring several famous ships from British and American history, including the Grand Turk and the USS Constitution. The ships remained for decades, but the types of products Old Spice sold changed with the times. From the 1940s through the 1960s, it primarily sold scented shaving soap and aftershave lotions. When P&G acquired Old Spice in 1990, it launched a whole new line of products, including body soaps, body washes and scented sprays.

The brand revamped its advertising and adopted a humorous approach. One tagline for its shower gel read: "The original. If your grandfather hadn't worn it, you wouldn't exist." But despite lots of marketing support from its new owner, the Old Spice business foundered. By 2006, it was losing out to Gillette, Palmolive, and Axe. Current users were getting old and younger users didn't want to be associated with such a dated brand.

During the struggles, however, the Old Spice team came across one intriguing consumer insight: More than 60 % of Old Spice products were purchased by women for the men in their lives. That had some interesting marketing possibilities, since the competition, especially Axe, focused completely on selling to men. In 2008, Old Spice hired ad agency Wieden + Kennedy to come up with a new advertising campaign. It was launched during the Super Bowl in 2010 and was entitled "The Man Your Man Could Smell Like." The commercial was geared directly toward women. Combined with an innovative online and social media campaign, it quickly became a cultural hit, and sales took off. Suddenly everyone was talking about a brand from the 1930s that their grandfather had used. (⬇ Online Exhibit 12.4)

As a follow-up to the initial TV commercials, the agency had the star of the Old Spice ads—former NFL player and actor Isaiah Mustafa—respond to requests sent to him via Twitter, Instagram, Facebook and YouTube. (⬇ Online Exhibit 12.5) The agency produced more than 180 YouTube videos during three days of intense shooting, which generated a massive response online. In the first 24 hours after the videos' release, the social media campaign generated almost six million YouTube views, more than President Obama's 2008 victory speech achieved in its first 24 hours. By day two, the Old Spice YouTube channel had eight of the eleven most popular videos on the internet. The numbers grew to 20 million at the end of the first week and more than 40 million by the end of the second week.

Twitter followers increased by 2,700 % and Facebook followers went from 500,000 to 800,000. By the end of the year, Old Spice sales had increased by 125 %, and it was now the best-selling body wash for men. The Old Spice business has grown by double digits every year since.

FIGURE 12.4
The ABCDE Grid for Old Spice's "The Man Your Man Could Smell Like"

Audience	Women who are buying body washes and deodorants for the men in their lives.
• Audience Insight	Women buy most of men's body washes and deodorants and could be influenced as to which brand they purchase.
Behavioral Objectives	Regain market share for Old Spice in the body wash and deodorant categories and grow overall Old Spice sales.
Content	
• Benefit	You'll love the way your man smells when he uses Old Spice. It's simply wonderful!
• Reason to Believe	Old Spice has the heritage and background to deliver a pleasant experience to both males and females.
• Tone/Character	Manly, confident, humorous.
Delivery—Media	"The Man Your Man Could Smell Like"
Delivery—Message	"Quite possibly the purest maple syrup on earth."
• On Brand	Tied to rugged manly heritage.
• Recognizable	Clever use of Old Spice logo and nautical imagery.
• Simple	Strong male spokespersons represent the brand.
• Attention Grabbing	Clever use of humor.
Evaluation	Sales of Old Spice and share of body wash and deodorant markets.

It's not creative unless it sells

Whether you sell sailing trips, maple syrup, four-wheel-drive vehicles, or body wash, it's critical to deeply understand your target audience and what will motivate them to buy your product. If you do your homework and get the right creative resources together, you can use the ABCDE Model to accomplish an array of amazing things that help build your company, launch a new premium product, engage a newly discovered niche audience, or rebound from a period of sluggish sales.

Three Keys to Effective Marketing across Culture, Country and Time

Rob Malcolm
Former Global President of Marketing, Sales and Innovation at Diageo

Think local: Everything begins at the local level. It starts with finding the business/customer opportunity—locally. Then you must find the most powerful insight about customers' motivation. This drives everything else. You must immerse yourself/your company in the local culture. You need to walk in the locals' shoes. As David Ogilvy observed, "Nothing is so powerful as an insight into human nature, what compulsions drive a man, what instincts dominate his action, even though his language often camouflages what really motivates him."

Act global: For a global or international company, determining the optimal "global approach" to winning, based on what creates the highest value for the company, is essential. This relies on the determination of the core competitive advantages—e.g., economies of scale, transnational innovation, marketing benefits, organizational benefits—all driven by what is needed to win with the customer. This will vary dramatically across industries. It affects how you organize (e.g., around geography, function, technology), what kind of talent you need (local, international, global, matrix) and how you make decisions.

Act local: Nelson Mandela's wisdom pertains here: "If you talk to a man in a language he understands, that goes to his head. If you talk to him in *his* language, that goes to his *heart*." All winning execution is local, even if it happens to be similar across geographies. Your offer may need to be tailored— don't be afraid to do that. Your engagement—communication and connections— must reflect local habits and cultural norms. In her insightful book, "Global Marketing and Advertising: Understanding Cultural Paradoxes," Marieke de Mooij observes: "The innate need for cross-situational consistency of Western marketing managers induces them to develop consistent brand identities and uniform advertising across countries. This is a fundamental error that may limit cross-cultural success." ■

CHAPTER 13

Non-Business Case Studies

> "Leadership is about finding your unique blueprint and expressing that courageously, confidently, and vulnerably."
>
> —Jennifer Mulholland

Virtually all our Marketing College students have had roles in government, nonprofits, or nongovernmental organizations (NGOs). Few had any business experience prior to occupying their public-sector or NGO roles. One of the biggest challenges when teaching them the ABCDE Model is translating the examples we use, because we draw almost all of them from the private sector. Transposing those experiences and examples into their worlds has been challenging, but we have become better at it over time.

Because of that challenge, we decided to put some extra focus on a separate chapter that presents examples of the ABCDE Model drawn directly from these public-sector and nonprofit segments. As we continue to gain traction, we will get more and more successful examples to share, and we welcome examples from our readers, as well. (You can send examples to info@craftingpersuasion.com.)

> *As we did in the last chapter each of these case studies uses a grid to organize the ABCDE communication model and make it easier to share with others as well as to help you make sure you cover all the strategic questions. We have posted a downloadable version of this grid for you to use on our website www.craftingpersuasion.com. We encourage you to use it as well.*

Case Study: Heroes Build in Tunisia

As you might recall from the introduction, concerns about violent extremism and the global perception of the United States prompted Kip's first meeting at the White House in 2008 and the eventual launch of the Marketing College. Little wonder, then, that violent extremism has become one of the most frequently raised topics in our Marketing College sessions over the years. Many of the cases our students work on focus on this issue. One, in particular, has become a template for other students as they prepare their own case presentations.

Some years ago, the small country of Tunisia was sending more fighters per capita to battle in Syria and Iraq than any other country with a substantial Muslim population. One student came to class with a difficult challenge: How could the U.S. government help the government of Tunisia dissuade these young men from joining the ongoing wars?

Unfortunately, in a one-week course, student teams do not have time to thoroughly research their case—to understand their audience thoroughly, develop thoughtful insights, and then translate those insights into powerful messages. So, over the course of the class, we ask them to develop a hypothesis they can test once they return to their roles.

We can do this for some of the tougher challenges because the cases we use in these sessions come from the students themselves. Students need to submit a difficult communications problem to be selected for the course. We select some of those cases and build teams around them—the case owner in each team has deep knowledge of the situation, and the rest of the team sets out to help that person solve their problem using the ABCDE Model.

The team assigned to the Tunisia problem worked through the ABCDE Model in an iterative way: establishing hypotheses, challenging them, then revisiting their earlier decisions. The ultimate objective, of course, was to reach the young men who had not yet left to fight. But how? Should they be reached directly or through influencers, peers, religious leaders, or family members? How broad should the target age range be? At what point were these young men beginning to head down the path to violent extremism? If we reached them too late and they had already decided to join, could we still dissuade them? If we reached them too early, before the message could take hold, would it even resonate?

Audience: The team decided to target a relatively broad group—urban males ages 13 to 25. They reasoned that the younger portion of the target were already being influenced by the older boys, and the older boys were being influenced by the young adults. Our local expert, who had worked in the country for years, described the conditions these young men faced and, in so doing, helped the group to develop initial insights to be tested. First, most of these young men had no jobs, as the country struggled economically. They had time on their hands to gather with their friends. They were a part of the hip-hop culture that was growing in the region, and they often listened to music as they hung out and talked. Often, they talked about the jihad. These young men were disengaged, and many of them had little or nothing to lose.

The second insight revealed a dichotomy. On the one hand, these young men were proud. Proud of their country. Proud of Tunisia's place in the Arab world. Tunisia's sense of identity was tied closely to its citizens' perception of themselves as the originators of the Arab Spring, the movement that overthrew despots and established new goals for Arab countries.

But just as they were proud about the leadership Tunisia had shown the world, most of these young men possessed little or no self-worth. Their sense of pride, their sense of belonging, and their sense of manhood was eroding. Their futures were devoid of hope, and they had little of which to be proud in the eyes of their family, friends and community.

For many of these young men, the call to arms had two big draws, and both would prove to be a source of new pride. First, they were being told they were fighting for a cause and would return to a hero's welcome.

Second, they would be paid. They would be able to contribute to the support of their families—again, a great source of pride. It didn't matter that neither of these things were true. A desperate man grabs hold of any source of hope. So, the team and its sponsor recognized that they would need to do additional research to understand their audience and better support their hypothesis.

Behavioral Objective: Experts on countering violent extremism theorize there are three times to "fight the fight" (i.e., try to dissuade youth from joining extremist organizations). First, you can wait until young people have already become violent extremists. You try to show them there is no glory in what they are doing; there are no rewards; they have been lied to. Not surprisingly, this approach has proven very ineffective. Second, you can inoculate young people before the lies take hold. If you can identify those at risk, this can be an effective strategy. Or third, you can identify individuals or groups that are in the process of being radicalized. They have already made a mental step toward extremism, so the goal is to redirect that anger and negative energy into a new, more positive outlet.

The Tunisia team chose to focus on this last approach. They would help these young men become heroes in the eyes of the people who mattered most to them and, in turn, become heroes in their own eyes. They would redefine what a hero looks like. Heroes don't destroy or tear down their world. Real heroes build up their communities. Real heroes use their energy to make a positive contribution to their people, their homes and their families. (⬇ Online Exhibit 13.1)

Content: The strategic statement was a *benefit promise* of recognition. People will be proud of you. You will be proud of yourself because you did something positive. The *reason these youth could believe* this promise was the fact that they and their Tunisian peers had changed the world before, during the Arab Spring. The *tone* of the campaign would be idealistic, upbeat and cool.

Delivery: The message was simple and recognizable. It was a statement made with conviction and idealism. Heroes Build. It would be on brand because the brand was Tunisia and these young men. It would be executed as a social media campaign with the focus on encouraging young people to come up with community service projects, followed by a video contest showcasing each project. That effort would be augmented by a hip-hop contest with artists competing to "show us you are building Tunisia." Weekly winners selected by the young people themselves would upload their videos on social media and go on the radio, all while vying for the grand prize—to perform in a free concert with recognized stars. To build the energy, there would be a series of massive graffiti art projects with professional artists guiding young artists. (⬇ Online Exhibit 13.2) The overarching theme was to search for hometown heroes and recognize them publicly and repeatedly. The program could be replicated and grow.

Evaluation: The ultimate metric was a reduction in young men leaving Tunisia to fight. Interim metrics to see if the public was becoming engaged included:

- The number of public-service-idea submissions and the week-to-week growth.
- The number of videos and hip-hop submissions.
- The number of people engaged in voting on the best ideas and artists.
- The number of graffiti projects and young artists involved.
- The number of concert attendees.

Here's what the Heroes Build strategy looked like when it was completed (Figure 13.1):

FIGURE 13.1	
The ABCDE Grid for Heroes Build	
Audience	Urban males ages 13–25.
• Audience Insight	These young men have lost hope and have little in their lives to be proud of. The jihad provides false hope that they can return from battle as heroes.
Behavioral Objectives	Reduce the number of young men who leave to fight by providing them with an alternative way to be seen as a hero.
Content	
• Benefit	If you turn away from the destructive and become a positive force in your community, you can change the world and will be recognized by those you value.
• Reason to Believe	Tunisian youth have changed the world before. You can do it again and create a new, lasting, positive change like the Arab Spring.
• Tone/Character	Idealistic, upbeat and cool.
Delivery—Media	The primary vehicles would be social media. Videos, Facebook posts, voting online.
Delivery—Message	Heroes Build
• On Brand	It must be clearly Tunisian.
• Recognizable	It is uniquely ours.
• Simple	The message is straightforward: Real men build.
• Attention Grabbing	Popular music and street art composed by Tunisian youth to tell the story of those who build.
Evaluation	Fewer fighters. More builders.

The Results: The owner of the case took it back to his ambassador and actually executed the program. Heroes Build was a competition designed to encourage individuals, groups, or associations to improve the country by volunteering. The public voted for the best projects through Facebook, YouTube, and a website. And the Heroes Build Best Projects received a reward that encouraged the winner to continue the project.

The Heroes Build project gave the people the opportunity to express themselves through their art and their vision of heroes and role models who inspire Tunisians. It inspired projects that included anything from simple gestures to help people in need—providing food, water, clothing, blankets, and other supplies—to classes created to help teach new languages, music, theater and other cultural, social, or sports-related skills. Youth volunteers repaired and spruced up public and private places, in some cases building new play areas or other sites and structures dedicated to young people. One interesting project aimed to "change a church as a cultural space." The author of the entry wrote:

> I am 25 years old rhythm guitarist, my project idea is to transform the old and abandoned church in Majaz al Bab as a cultural space [that] contains a coffee shop and cultural clubs to teach music, theater, painting, dance and music as the music and film and theatrical performance spaces.

The Embassy kickstarted and built momentum for the project with a series of concerts, advertising them to the Tunisian public through social media posts, such as this one:

> 22 April at 17:00
>
> **The 5th Build Heroes concert** with the presence of "Hatem Karoui" with her show "PASS-PORT" and the cast of local music "Under the Roots," mixture of Jazz, and Reggae Gnewa to "Tabarka Sky Lantern Festival - HELMA." Be present among us.

The organizers also sparked and expanded mobilization through graffiti in different regions of Tunisia. The U.S. Embassy awarded a grant to a group of high-profile Tunisian graffiti artists, called the Heroes Build Team, which went out and painted inspirational murals around the country. The murals were created in coordination with other events, including live debates and the concert series, with everything focused on promoting youth volunteerism. The murals caught on, and soon youth were creating their own murals around the country and submitting videos on the Embassy Facebook and YouTube channels showing their work.

The resulting enthusiasm has led to even more community-building and community-service projects. An elementary school teacher built a small theater for his students. High school kids led school clean-ups and construction projects. In one town, a group of kids volunteered to entertain the children at a pediatric hospital.

The program eventually resulted in more than 50 media placements in the first wave. All were positive, which is no small feat for the United States in Tunisia. The project became so popular that politicians, including the Minister of Defense and the Minister of Youth and Sports, have publicly praised it for promoting youth volunteerism.

Case Study: Anti-Smoking Campaign

Normally in case studies, we look back at a previous event or program for which we know the results. But you rarely have the luxury of going through that process when faced with a communication challenge. Nobody knows what will work. In this case study, we're going to develop a communications strategy together, just like you will have to. The end product in this case is a potential communications strategy that will need to be turned into executions and tested.

It wasn't that long ago that smoking in the United States was ubiquitous. People were permitted to smoke in restaurants, offices, even airplanes—well after the connection between smoking and cancer, heart disease, and all manner of deadly illnesses was common knowledge. In many parts of the world, smoking is still extremely common.

The people and organizations who took it upon themselves to try to stop this epidemic tried a wide range of messages to make their case and sway their audience. Some have worked—to an extent. Most didn't achieve their behavioral objective for many years, and smoking retains its hold on a diminished (though still significant) portion of the American public.

The facts compiled by the Centers for Disease Control and Prevention are dramatic and undeniable:

- Smoking leads to disease and disability and harms nearly every organ of the body.
- Smoking is the leading cause of preventable death.
- The tobacco industry spends billions of dollars each year on cigarette advertising and promotions.
- 37.8 million people—15.5 % of all adults (17.5 % of males, 13.5 % of females)—were cigarette smokers in 2016.
- Cigarette smoking is responsible for more than 480,000 deaths per year in the United States, including more than 41,000 deaths resulting from secondhand smoke exposure. This is about one in five deaths annually, or 1,300 deaths every day.
- Thousands of young people start smoking cigarettes every day.
- Many adult cigarette smokers want to quit smoking.
- On average, smokers die 10 years earlier than nonsmokers.
- If current trends continue, 5.6 million Americans younger than 18 years of age today are expected to die prematurely from a smoking-related illness.

As with the effort to curb violent extremism, we can consider a few approaches. Let's start with the theory that it might be effective to divert young people before they pick up this bad habit. Teens have long been a target of the tobacco companies. Young people ages 12 to 17 are the most likely to start smoking. Nine out of 10 smokers start before they are 18. Tobacco companies know that getting them hooked early is one of the best ways to make a loyal smoker for life. According to the CDC, each day more than 3,200 children younger than 18 smoke their first cigarette. And an estimated 2,100 youngsters and young adults who have been occasional smokers become daily smokers every day. Tobacco companies have been targeting teens for generations, and while the government has tried to curb some marketing specifically aimed at young people, the industry is pretty clever.

We discussed the development of the adolescent mind in Chapter 9, noting that young people are not as logical as they will be when they grow older. Facts and figures do not sway their decisions. Most young people think they can quit smoking easily. Further, they think the health consequences of smoking don't apply to them. There was a time, not very long ago, when smoking was a rite of passage. Youth embraced smoking to express rebellion and exhibit evidence of maturity. And it was cool. The desire to belong, combined with a feeling of invincibility, often meant that being cool was critical and death was something that only happened to old people.

One insight important for this exercise is the fact that attitudes appear to be changing. A study by the University of California San Francisco and the Stanford University School of Medicine found that fewer young people plan to smoke or think smoking makes them look mature. In the last dozen years, California teens have come to see smoking as riskier and less socially acceptable. More and more, they perceive smoking as an activity that will lead to health complications, such as heart attacks and lung cancer. Perhaps the constant drumbeat of the deadly results of smoking has begun to take hold. (⬇ Online Exhibit 13.3) Perhaps more young people have observed firsthand the damage smoking has done to the health of their own family or friends. Whatever the reason, evidence suggests that the historical motives for smoking among young people have begun to change.

So, if you were charged with the responsibility of stopping teenage smoking, what strategy would you develop? As of now, the approach continues to be the same as that aimed at adults—scare them straight—and it might be working. But is there another way? Let's run it through the ABCDE Model and see what we find.

Audience: Perhaps we should start when preteens are just beginning to experiment with smoking—say, around age 12. Starting younger might be a possibility, but scaring younger children might spark a public backlash. We should explore that, but let's start with 12-year-olds. Since the research indicates that young people ages 12 to 18 are the early triers, perhaps that is the best target for our diversion efforts. For our audience *insight*, we could consider the hypothesis is that teens are beginning to turn away from smoking as a means of rebellion or as a sign of maturity. It appears that the cool factor might be waning. It's only a hypothesis with some early research support, but it seems worthy of a communications test.

Behavioral Objective: Again, it would seem pretty straightforward—steer our target audience away from ever starting to smoke. But understanding the adolescent mind, there is probably a second, equally important behavior to consider: Getting teens to convince their peers that smoking is decidedly not cool. This behavior will dovetail with our reason to believe, detailed below.

Content: The *benefit promise* probably needs to include a promise of a longer, healthier life that will make both the audience and the people who love them happier. But that can't be the only promise, because that has been the promise for years. We need to find a way to convince this audience that *not* smoking is the new cool thing to do, and that if they smoke they will somehow be left out by their peers. The idea is to use the brain development insights we've gained to give us leverage with this audience that cares so much about what their peers think.

The *reason to believe*, then, will be critical. We can use all kinds of health data, which appears to be having some impact on this audience, but the other half of our story remains problematic. We probably can't use facts and figures to undo the cool factor. We need to depend on other reasons to believe. Star power might be one possibility. Given how important imitation and the affinity for celebrities tends to be for this age group, perhaps having highly regarded celebrities speaking to the "new cool" could have some impact. But in the end, peer influence and peer pressure could be the real key, and the leverage of social media could be the way to accelerate it.

Finally, the *tone and character* of the campaign might have different dimensions. On the one hand, we want this to be serious without being preachy. It can't be adults talking down to these young people. But alternatively, it is possible that a little humor in some of the executions could be very effective with this audience. This needs to be tested.

Delivery—Media: Social media appears ideal for this communication effort. We can test alternative vehicles, alternative messages, and alternative celebrities. We need to get the ball rolling and see if young people take up the challenge. We might take some lessons from an existing effort highlighted in a 2014 *New York Times* story. (⬇ Online Exhibit 13.4) The article looked at attempts to engage teens with a somewhat different but equally interesting anti-smoking approach. In 2000, a campaign called "Truth" was launched that called on tobacco companies to tell the truth about the terrible effects of smoking. The newer campaign, dubbed "Finish It," built off its predecessor. Both campaigns turned on the insight that teens want to be agents of change. While the original campaign tapped into the rebellious nature of young people, the newer campaign took a subtler approach, while still encouraging young people to use their social media clout to rally their peers and friends against smoking.

Delivery—Message: We need to develop a core message and then consider alternative executions to test. We can use A/B testing to see which messages, celebrities, facts, etc., generate the best results. As we create the messaging, we need to test it against our criteria. Have we created an "ownable," recognizable message and execution so that each new version builds on the previous one? While simplicity is important in any marketing campaign, crafting simple, attention-grabbing messages is even more critical here because we are focusing our efforts on social media. What's our big idea? What's our big picture? What can we do that will be arresting in the first five seconds to get our audience to read further or continue watching?

Given the background we've provided, perhaps a communication strategy for this marketing might look something like this. What would you change?

FIGURE 13.2
The ABCDE Grid for Our Hypothetical Anti-Smoking Campaign

Audience	Young people ages 12 to 18 who are potential smokers.
• Audience Insight	Even smokers wish they could stop. Getting to them before they start might halt this epidemic within a generation. In addition, young people are starting to recognize that smoking cigarettes is no longer the cool thing to do.
Behavioral Objectives	Don't even think about smoking cigarettes. And stop your friends from smoking as well.
Content	
• Benefit	You and your loved ones will be better off if you never start smoking. But the big point is that the cool thing to do is *not* smoke.
• Reason to Believe	In addition to the overwhelming evidence of the harmful health effects from smoking as well as secondhand smoke, you will be shunned by your friends. Celebrities *and* your friends say so.
• Tone/Character	Serious but not preachy. But test humor.
Delivery—Media	This is a social media effort. It reaches the audience and is the most trusted way for kids to talk to kids.
Delivery—Message	
• On Brand	
• Recognizable	The message would need to be developed, including the "brand," as part of the strategic communication plan.
• Simple	
• Attention Grabbing	
Evaluation	Number of young people ages 12 to 18 who don't start smoking each year. Number of teens who engage on social media about the evils of smoking.

Case Studies: Iconic Public Service Campaigns

Some public-service, nonprofit communications campaigns proved so effective that many of us, if asked, would swear they are still on the air. As an exercise, deconstruct these campaigns and see if you can determine the communications strategies that led to their development. We encourage you to use the ABCDE Grid, which you can find at www.craftingpersuasion.com, to guide your analysis.

This is your brain on drugs

This campaign was launched by the Partnership for a Drug Free America in 1987. The phrase became a part of the vernacular, and the imagery was visceral—the frying pain as drugs, and an egg cracked into it and frying as your brain on drugs. (⬇ Online Exhibit 13.5) While critics have challenged the effectiveness of the campaign and the accuracy of the metaphor, it is regarded as one of the most memorable public-service campaigns ever.

Go through the model. Who do you think was the audience? What was the behavioral objective? The content? Judge how effective the campaign was—remember, this came out in a world before social-media existed. How did it fare in terms of being on brand, recognizable, simple, attention grabbing, and memorable?

You could learn a lot from a dummy

This campaign was introduced in 1985 at a time when getting people to wear seatbelts was still a major challenge. While there are still holdouts, things are much better today. In 1985, seatbelt usage was at 42%. In 2017, it was at 90%. The U.S. Department of Transportation's ad agency turned crash test dummies into personalities who demonstrated just what happens in even the smallest crash. (⬇ Online Exhibit 13.6) Again, process this through the steps of the ABCDE Model, and decide whether it was as effective as it was memorable.

Friends don't let friends drive drunk

This campaign started in 1983. (⬇ Online Exhibit 13.7) It goes beyond a flat-footed platitude that you should not drink and drive. What do you think the insight was that produced this phrase that has become part of our lexicon? This campaign was so effective that, since it began to air, nearly 70% of Americans have reported that they've tried to prevent a friend from driving after drinking too much, and it has led to the concept of the designated driver.

People start pollution. People can stop it.

While littering certainly hasn't been eliminated, today it's rare to see somebody toss a bag of trash out the car window as they speed down the highway. There was a time when this practice was commonplace. This campaign launched on the first Earth Day, in 1971, and Ad Age Magazine named it one of the 100 best advertising campaigns of the 20th century. (⤓ Online Exhibit 13.8) By the end of the Keep America Beautiful campaign, litter had been reduced by as much as 88% in 300 communities across 38 states.

Only you can prevent forest fires

Like so many of these great public-service campaigns, Smokey the Bear was created by the U.S. Ad Council. (⤓ Online Exhibit 13.9) Smokey arrived in 1944 and has been lodged in the American consciousness ever since— even though he is rarely seen anymore. What would have led a creative team to come up with this character and campaign?

Just because you are not selling a product or a service, you are still trying to persuade some audience, somewhere to change a behavior—a behavior that is valuable to your organization. The ABCDE Model is a proven tool to help you improve your success rate in accomplishing your objectives.

So, while these iconic public service campaigns underscore the power of an effective message, by reverse engineering them and going through the case studies in this chapter, it also becomes apparent just how effective the ABCDE communication model can be when applied to communication strategies outside the typical business sphere. That flexibility and the elegant simplicity of the model allows professionals who work for nonprofits and government agencies to bring a new level of rigor, preparation, and effectiveness to their communication efforts.

How to Create Loyalty Among Non-Loyal Audiences

Kelly Hlavinka
Loyalty Consultant, Strategist and Practitioner

Regardless of what industry sector you are in, it is likely that you have a small, die-hard group of customers who already are very loyal. Like most companies, though, you probably also have a much bigger group of customers who have a fickle—or even fragile—relationship with you. Fostering deeper relationships with that second group of customers requires strategic focus and excellent execution. But, what are the right areas to focus on to accomplish that?

1. **The starting point—providing fair consideration:** Let's face it—enticing a customer to engage more with your company in a highly cluttered marketplace starts with an economic incentive. Whether it is a discount, points, miles, or free shipping, extending a value proposition that shows a customer that *'I get my money's worth'* is the most effective way to break through. By starting with such "hard benefits," you can add as many as 5 to 10 percentage points to the annual value of your engaged customers, according to a ValuTalk white paper from COLLOQUY.

2. **The important missed dimension—engaging** customers on an emotional level: Too many companies pursue customer loyalty by deploying only the first element: economic and transactional rewards. For their engagement to be sustainable, however, it is critical to blend in elements that show a customer you *value their importance* through personalized perks, privileges, and recognition of their important status to your organization. When delivered in a thoughtful and tailored manner, 80% of customers say they are likely to be more loyal, according to Epsilon's 2017 *Power of Me* study. Researchers at the University of Southern California found the lure even among Millennials, with 85% of respondents in that demographic saying that personalized recognition is critical to earning their loyalty.

3. **The new expectation—**let me engage as I want to: Creating loyalty means being available to your customers in any channel they choose. Whether that is their smart phone, tablet, or talking to a real human being in person, their expectation is that *you* will be ready and able to help *them*. It also means ceding control to your customers. Today, your

customers expect you to enable them to easily share their experience with your company via reviews, ratings, and social media. Meanwhile, the way customers prefer to engage with companies continues to evolve. A report from Crowdtwist suggests that roughly a third of Millennials and Gen Z customers prefer to engage by playing games, such as the initiatives that Chipotle, Ford, and others have created.

The bottom line

It really comes down to this: Is your experience seamless and easy? How your customers feel when they engage with your company is the ultimate test. Do you make it smooth and simple? If not, economic rewards, personalized perks, and omni-channel availability won't add up to customer loyalty. The combination of those factors with a frictionless experience is what will create higher emotional engagement with your company. As Capgemini research suggests, 82% of customers say high emotional engagement is what creates real loyalty. ■

CHAPTER 14

Heads Up— Common Pitfalls to Avoid

> "Success is the result of hard work, learning from failure, and persistence."
> –Colin Powell

The game of chess can be taught to a beginner in about an hour, and yet requires a lifetime to master. The same can be said of the ABCDE Communication Model. It's a common sense approach to creating a communication strategy and execution plan. You can learn the basics in about an hour. And yet, to do communication strategy well takes a lot of effort, thought, and practice. Like chess, mastering it can be the work of a lifetime, and you can always improve on your ability to craft a well-considered communication strategy.

In this chapter we will cover things to watch out for as you begin to implement the ABCDE Model. With enough time and effort, recognizing these pitfalls will become more like second nature, and you will gain an expertise for creating communication strategies that will benefit you throughout your life.

Don't lose sight of the core principles

As we've mentioned multiple times throughout this book, you should always develop a solid communication goal and strategy that has buy-in and support from your team *before you do any execution.* Over years of working with teams from around the world, we've observed that people have a strong urge to do execution before developing a proper communication strategy. Why? We've come up with several explanations. You should be aware of and watch out for these tendencies in your own work.

Bias for short-term over long-term results

Diplomats stationed in various embassies around the world feel pressure to respond to what the current ambassador wants. Whether a call for an immediate press release, Facebook post, or tweet, you typically do not have the opportunity to push back on those requests when you work in such a demanding role. It takes a lot of courage, not to mention a willingness to accept some potential career damage, to ask: "Why are we doing this?"

The time to create your communication strategy, whether you're working for a U.S. embassy or your local Parent Teacher Association, is *not* in the heat of the moment. That rarely works. Instead, take the time in advance to think about what you're really trying to accomplish. Who are you trying to reach? What key message do you want to deliver? Why should your audience believe it? How are you going to evaluate the results? All these decisions will take time to reflect upon, discuss, and eventually agree on. They can't be answered with the appropriate thought and consideration when every five minutes you have someone asking, "Have you sent out that new Facebook post yet?" You need to get management buy-in for a responsible strategy before that short-term pressure comes down.

While it might be safer and more satisfying to "do something *now*"— and it might keep your boss happy in the moment—the results from this type of frantic effort are typically short-lived and often detrimental since they aren't part of a long-term, well-crafted messaging strategy.

Difficulty of getting team alignment in advance

Not only does it take time to craft a proper communication strategy, it also takes hard work to get everyone to provide their input and then throw their support behind it. If you take the time to build buy-in, there are going to be numerous and sometimes heated debates about what should go into your communication strategy (and, just as important, what should be kept out).

For example, just getting everyone to agree on your target audience can be a challenge. It's so much faster and easier to just get started with execution. It feels like you're making progress in getting your message out, but don't be fooled! When the time comes to assess how you're doing, you will probably run into numerous arguments and disagreements about just how much you're progressing—assuming you are progressing at all, which is highly unlikely when you play the "ready, shoot, aim" game. In that scenario, some on your team might think you're doing great, while others see the results as disappointing. This is because you never took the time in the beginning to get agreement on your overall communication strategy before you got underway with execution.

A good analogy for this process is planning a family road trip, which typically involves an in-depth, pre-trip discussion with all your family members about where you want to go, what you want to do and experience, which route you want to take, and what you want the overall outcome to be. You probably will have a lot of back and forth, maybe even some arguments, with various family members on all these issues. But you really should take the time to air out these issues and attempt consensus before you all climb into the family car. At least get to the point where the parents can make a final call: "This is what we're doing" Otherwise, no one in that car will have any idea where they are going. You'll be making great time going the wrong direction. Good luck with that!

The pitfalls at each step along the way

Each phase of the ABCDE Model presents its own challenges. Beyond remaining aware of and avoiding these problems from the outset, you need to remain wary of the smaller but equally troublesome issues that arise within each of these stages. Some pitfalls we can learn only from experience, and some challenges are unique to each individual situation, but we can identify many of the ones that are common to most communicators.

Audience: News flash—you're not it

The most common mistake people make in implementing a communication strategy is confusing who your target audience is. It's way too easy to see the world solely from your own perspective and emphasize what you think your target audience needs to know and what you think would be most persuasive. That rarely turns out well.

Trying to see the world from another person's point of view does not come easily to most people. It takes hard work, during which time you'll need to continually challenge your assumptions. It requires time-consuming, in-depth research done by marketing research professionals to really try to understand your target audience and remain as objective as possible while developing those insights. How do *they* feel about an issue? Why? What are *they* open to listening to? What are *they* not willing to listen to? Until you thoroughly ground yourself in your target audience's perspective, you will have trouble making any real connection with them. You risk not truly understanding what will work and not work with your audience, and why.

No matter how you define your target audience, you will need to park your personal assumptions at the door when you start crafting your communication strategy. Get to know them and keep asking "why" until you feel very comfortable that you can start to see the world through their eyes. It's harder than it sounds.

You cannot stop once you get to this level of target audience insights, either. You need to continually find ways to share your thinking with them and get their reaction to possible messaging. Do they understand what you're trying to communicate? How can you adapt your message to make it easier for them to follow what you're trying to share? Try to gain a deeper and deeper understanding of what they want to hear. Keep refining your sense of why they believe what they believe (and how strongly they believe this) before you try to change anything.

And recognize that some of their beliefs are so fundamental they will *not* change regardless of what you do or say. You cannot afford to put your audience on the defensive. Once you do, you might as well forget about getting them to your desired behavior.

Behavioral objectives—That which gets measured gets done

Most communicators make the same two mistakes. First, they do not or cannot measure their behavioral objective. Second, they come up with too many objectives. Let's take a close look at both of these problems.

In Chapter 4, we discussed the various ways you could define a behavioral objective. We emphasized the critical need for behavioral data and having the means to gather it in a timely and affordable manner. Some behavioral objectives are easy enough to measure, such as sales or client growth. You should already have the means to gather that sort of information relatively quickly. In addition, you can compare how this data is trending so you can do a deeper analysis of all the various factors that might be influencing your behavioral objective.

Sometimes, though, it's not that simple. If your behavioral objective is to get the general population to support and vote for members of Congress who support Medicare for All legislation, you need to invest quite a bit in ongoing polling data. As we all know, this kind of information can sometimes be flawed or misleading. It can be hard to measure your behavioral objective on local issues, as well. Imagine you are concerned about motorists who are speeding through residential areas. You want to create a communication campaign to get them to slow down. What would be an appropriate behavioral objective? Ideally, it would be to measure a change in attitude among all drivers about the importance of slowing down, along with a drop in their average speed. But getting this data would be time-consuming and costly.

So, you might have to get creative in defining what success looks like. In the anti-speeding campaign, tracking the number of speeding tickets issued in a residential area over time might make a more realistic behavioral objective. If your campaign works, you should expect to see a drop in speeding tickets—ideally compared with the number of tickets in a similar neighborhood that doesn't get the communication. This could help indicate whether your anti-speeding message had the desired impact.

The second big mistake—having too many objectives—typically happens when you attempt to get everyone on the team to agree on strategy. An example of an objective with too many components might resemble a product launch with specific targets for increased market share, sales,

profits, and breakeven points in a set of specific time frames. While you
realistically can achieve any one of those objectives in a certain period of
time, achieving *all* of them simultaneously is far less likely. You're probably going to have to make some tradeoffs. For example, you might need to
invest more in marketing to grow market share, which in turn will reduce
profits and delay your breakeven point.

To use a non-business example, go back to the neighborhood speeding
scenario. Imagine a set of behavioral objectives that sought to "significantly reduce the number of speeding tickets issued to motorists who drive
through our neighborhoods while increasing the number of voters willing
to support lower posted speed limits in our city." Such a behavioral objective might hope to address both short-term and long-term issues, but the
team working on this problem would be better served if they had a single
behavioral objective. They could focus on making that happen, and then
roll out a new campaign in the future with an updated, single objective.

Content—Keep it simple, stupid (K.I.S.S.)

Recall that the content portion of the ABCDE Model is comprised of a)
benefit, b) reason to believe and c) tone and character. Most communicators try to squeeze too much into one or more of these elements.

In the 1960s, the U.S. Navy adopted a fundamental design principle
dubbed K.I.S.S., or "Keep It Simple, Stupid." Kelly Johnson, the Navy
officer who came up with K.I.S.S., was an engineer by training and had
enormous respect for his profession. He didn't consider his peers stupid;
he just wanted to stress the point that the simpler you can keep things in
design, the greater your chances for a successful execution or deployment
of the airplane or ship you are building.

The same holds true when creating content for your communication
strategy. You are much better off having a single benefit—or, at a minimum, a primary and secondary benefit—rather than setting out to provide
multiple benefits. You will be more persuasive with a single, powerful benefit and related reason to believe than you will with a litany of them. More
is *not* better. As a case in point, consider these two benefit statements
developed for Crest Toothpaste:

1. *Crest Toothpaste helps prevent cavities because it has a special ingredient (Fluoristan) and is endorsed by the American Dental Association.*

2. *Crest Toothpaste helps prevent cavities, protects your gums, freshens your breath and whitens your teeth because it has a number of special ingredients (Fluoristan, Scope mouthwash, whitening elements) and is endorsed by the American Dental Association.*

The first statement is the one Crest used when Procter & Gamble launched the product in the 1960s. The message illustrated a single-minded focus on preventing cavities and noted that Crest was endorsed by the American Dental Association (ADA), the first toothpaste to get such a designation. This positioning and communication strategy enabled Crest to become the leading brand of toothpaste in the United States, and it retains that position today. The second statement covers a number of additional features that various Crest products offer today, but these are all sold as "flankers" to the original Crest brand. These newer products with additional features still trade on the heritage and trust consumers already have in Crest. But if the brand had launched with all this at once, it probably would have confused consumers, and Crest might not have achieved the business success it's had over the past 60 years.

Similarly, you should aim to define your tone or brand character in as few words as possible, even one if you can distill it that clearly. Why? In a practical sense, the more words you have the more difficult it becomes to create executions (e.g., TV ads, social media campaigns, print ads, etc.) that can consistently and powerfully communicate your chosen tone to the target audience. Think about some of the brands you admire or use: If you tried to describe their brand personality to someone who had never heard of them, would you need a whole page of words to describe the brand's personality?

- Crest: factual, professional, dependable
- BMW: masculine, powerful, serious
- Red Bull: youthful, energetic, irreverent
- Tesla: innovative, smart, progressive
- Rolex: elegant, dependable, classic
- McDonald's: friendly, affordable, fun

Take a moment to try it. Think of a couple of your favorite brands and select three words to describe their tone and character. Do you really need more than three to get the job done? While additional words might help round out the picture, you can see how adding more words begins to dilute what makes a brand special and unique.

Again, it's better to just Keep It Simple, Stupid. When you're creating content, give it a K.I.S.S—no more than a single benefit and a single reason to believe. When defining your tone and character, do it with a K.I.S.S— three powerful words are enough. If you can craft the right combination of focused benefit, reason to believe and tone/character, and then remain focused on those, you will dramatically increase your odds of creating and growing a powerful brand and/or communication campaign.

Delivery—Pigs get fat, hogs get slaughtered

As the old fat pigs and slaughtered hogs adage suggests, we tend to embrace ambition but risk losing it all when we get greedy. Keep that mantra in mind when deciding what you want to include as the delivery piece of your overall communication strategy. Think carefully about how many different media channels you want your campaign message to go through. While Hootsuite and other tools can help you to manage multiple media channels efficiently, remember that each media channel you use requires a certain amount of care and maintenance to make sure it remains an effective part of your overall media plan.

To start, make sure you have a thorough understanding of your target audience's media consumption habits. Twitter is an effective social media platform, but only if the audience you are interested in uses and refers to it on a regular basis. How does your target audience use media? How much? How often? And for what? Which delivery channels? Once you have a deep understanding of what your target audience typically con- sumes and how and where they like to consume it, you'll have a sound basis for determining which and how many channels to include in your communication strategy.

The size of your budget will dictate some of these choices, of course. Traditional media channels (e.g., network and cable television ads, print, outdoor, radio, etc.) can quickly run into millions of dollars, especially if you try to get your message out to a national audience. Today, companies often spend even larger sums on Google and Facebook advertising. No matter how big your media budget is, it never seems like enough. And don't be fooled into thinking there are any free delivery channels—even if you're not paying for the cost of distribution, you still have the costs of creating the content you utilize.

Speaking of content, you'll need to create and release fresh content on a regular basis. There is no greater cause for concern about the quality of a brand and its message than to go to a Facebook or Instagram page and see that the last update was posted months ago. Depending on the category and the channel, you will need to plan on posting fresh content at least once a week, once a day, or maybe even several times a day. Every day...every week...every month...every year...forever! Are you sure you're prepared to do that?

You also need to monitor the various media channels you are on. If you create a communication strategy for your business, you should set a maximum amount of time you will permit before replying to a consumer comment or complaint. That means someone on your team or an outside party will need to check that channel on a regular basis. (Watch out especially for spammers—they can create havoc in a short amount of time if left unchecked.) Think through how you plan to respond to public comments, as well, because many social media channels don't allow you to simply delete comments unless they violate specific user agreements, such as prohibitions against profanity. Besides, if consumers view your media channel as censored or lacking in transparency, it's going to reflect poorly on your brand or business.

As you consider all these questions, remember not to get greedy. Pigs get fat and hogs get slaughtered, so think carefully about how many delivery channels you really want to use. Fewer is typically better than more. Make sure you have the budget and manpower not only to get started in these media channels, but to stay on top of them with fresh content and quick response times, as well.

Evaluation—An unexamined campaign is not worth doing

The last part of the ABCDE Model is arguably the most critical to the entire process. A communication strategy is never "done." The overall environment changes. Consumer attitudes evolve. Opinions shift. Unanticipated events occur. All of this will impact your communication strategy—and that's before you even take the time and effort to evaluate how your latest campaign is doing. But the biggest mistake a communicator can make is skipping or shortchanging the evaluation process because they get busy or distracted, move on to other projects and priorities, or to avoid any kind of assessment because things haven't gone as originally planned.

Even if the truth might appear uglier than you fear, and even if it might reflect poorly on your efforts, resist these excuses. You put in the effort to craft your strategy. You studied your target audience. You debated and agreed on what the behavioral objective should be. You and your team or agency developed what you believed to be a compelling messaging, with a clearly defined benefit, reason to believe and tone and character. You took care to pick the best way to deliver your message. The least you can do now is go back and evaluate how it performed.

What worked? What didn't? Why did it succeed or fall short of your goal? What would you do differently the next time? What adjustments would you make? Did you have the right behavioral objective? Did the message resonate with the target audience? Were you satisfied with your mix of delivery channels?

You can't just measure the results and leave it there; you have to determine the reasons behind the results. If your campaign worked and you don't know why, you can't repeat it or build on it. If it didn't work and you don't know why, you can neither fix it nor avoid the same mistakes next time. By taking the time and effort to evaluate your campaign's performance, your own performance *will* improve over time. Sure, you might get lucky and have success with your messaging the first time out with a new campaign. But don't count on it. Embrace your mistakes for what they can teach you. With the right discipline and effort, you can make significant progress, even against the most challenging communication problem.

Communication strategy: Use it or lose it!

Congratulations! You have a communication strategy! Now you need to put it to work, or else all that effort goes for naught.

What do we mean by putting your strategy to work? Simply this: Any time there is any development of any execution for a campaign, you need work to make sure everyone has a copy of the communication strategy and understands it. Before reviewing any creative from anyone, whether internal or from an outside agency, start the meeting with a quick review of the communication strategy and remind everyone there what the creative message should try to communicate. If you think the creative is off strategy, even if you fall in love with the execution, say so and explain why. Then make sure that the folks revising it understand the issue or issues that need to be addressed.

Why is this process important? Let's return to that dream house you were building in Chapter 1. You hired the greatest architect since Frank Lloyd Wright. You have the perfect location and the very best materials. You have the money in the bank to pay for all of it. With construction about to start, wouldn't you want to know that plans were in place to build your house precisely as the architect designed it? If mistakes occurred after the project was underway, wouldn't you want to make sure they were addressed in a timely manner? When the house was all finished, wouldn't you want to evaluate the finished product to make sure it aligned with what you originally envisioned and designed?

Of course you would, and your communication campaign should be no different. Brilliant blueprints enable builders to create beautiful buildings. Thoughtful communication strategies enable teams to launch and sustain powerful, persuasive messages that move audiences to action.

But only if you stick to your communication strategy every time.

How to Guard Against Someone Hijacking Your Message

Klon Kitchen
Senior Fellow, Technology, National Security, and Science at The Heritage Foundation

Communications is not war. However, we can gain insights into how to better communicate *from* war—particularly counterinsurgency strategy. Take, for example, a bit of wisdom from David Galula, one of the most accomplished counterinsurgency strategists and practitioners of the early 20th century. In his book "Counterinsurgency Warfare: Theory and Practice," Galula wrote:

> *"The asymmetrical situation has important effects on propaganda. The insurgent, having no responsibility, is free to use every trick; if necessary, he can lie, cheat, exaggerate. He is not obliged to prove; he is judged by what he promises, not by what he does. Consequently, propaganda is a powerful weapon for him. With no positive policy but with good propaganda, the insurgent may still win.*

> *"The counterinsurgent is tied to his responsibilities and to his past, and for him, facts speak louder than words. He is judged on what he does, not on what he says. If he lies, cheats, exaggerates, and does not prove, he may achieve some temporary success, but at the price of being discredited for good."*

Here is the point: Those who want to hijack your message (insurgents) will typically enjoy an advantage because they are less bound to the truth and "the rules." Imagine you are the chief marketing officer for a brand-new line of premium cosmetics. The day before you roll out your six-month U.S. marketing campaign, a fringe animal rights group deploys its own marketing effort, accusing your company of testing perfume by spraying it into the eyes of fluffy white rabbits. These insurgents either don't know or are ignoring the fact that all of your cosmetics are developed in the European Union—where animal testing for cosmetics is banned—because they have decided to use your brand as a means to exert political pressure for a similar ban in the United States. What do you do?

Well, if you have not anticipated this contingency, your job is a lot harder than it has to be. All brand managers need to continually assess the intentions and capabilities of their most likely insurgents and to proactively prepare responses for their challenges. But, while this is necessary, it will not be sufficient.

The most fundamental step you can make to prevent someone from hijacking your message is to be coherent. It works like this: *influence* (i.e., the ultimate goal) is derived from *legitimacy* (i.e., brand trust), which is a product of *coherence* (i.e., consistency with your brand promise). Remember what Galula says: The insurgent is "judged by what he promises," while the counterinsurgent (you) is "judged on what he does." The critical decisions to protect and to defend your message will not be made after you have been attacked, but long before the insurgent makes his first move.

In the end, even strict coherence does not guarantee success against the insurgent, but the lack of coherence will guarantee failure. ■

CHAPTER 15

The Road Ahead

"The key to success is to get out into the store
and listen to what the associates have to say."

–Sam Walton

Sam Walton opened his first Walmart store in 1962 with a simple concept. He would listen to his customers and employees and provide them with the best value. He was famous for his Saturday meetings, his visits to every town, and his unending desire to gain an edge by listening to his people and the marketplace. The rest is history.

Today, we're barraged with a litany of new ideas and products promising to become "the next thing." Bitcoin, blockchain, artificial intelligence, bot networks, 5G—it all can be a bit overwhelming…until we remember what Sam taught us.

Listening is the key that unlocks ideas and innovation. It is our signpost on the road ahead. The only difference between 1962 and today is *how* we can listen. Now, data science is our ears. We can learn how humans behave or how artificial bot networks fool us. We can see why engagement occurs, how long it lasts, and whether it is merely building awareness or actually fostering loyalty. We can anticipate exactly what our audience desires before we write the first word of a new campaign.

We are entering an exciting new era of innovation in the fields of communication, marketing, and diplomacy. As these areas evolve and professionals in them become more sophisticated, we gain greater and greater precision—and with that, our ability to persuade improves dramatically.

If we were on a boat at sea in the middle of a storm, we would grab a harness and safely lock ourselves in before we piloted forward. Our version of a harness in a time of intense technological change and innovation is the ABCDE Model. Let's use it to look at what's ahead.

Audience

Analytics and Actionable Insights: Sam Walton would have hired more data scientists than any CEO on earth if he'd had access to the tools and technology we have today. Are you wearing the right set of glasses to see your marketplace? Do you know your data science team? Are you utilizing insights to better understand human behavior, how social media and internet sites are changing the world of media, and how we can harness data to give us insights? Are you ready to join us for the big bonfire in which we burn our useless accumulations of pie charts, slides, and reports?

Audience Architecture: Using data techniques, we can map out exactly how the PESO (paid, earned, shared, owned) media world is working today. We will be able to see how audience segments interact, how their journeys occur across multiple channels, and what the right PESO mix of media should be to consistently reach them. You'll know who influences a cardiologist or a journalist. You'll know which three social media channels are important for an audience segment and in what order to prioritize them. You'll realize how to spend less on advertising and more on paid media to move the right earned content to the right places. In subtle yet powerful ways, our ability to see how our audience acts will revolutionize how we reach them. The interdependencies they have with the people they follow, trust, and respect will become obvious.

Behavior

Improve on Current Models: If we assume all current media models are old school, we don't get defensive. We don't protect the past. And that's when breakthroughs can occur. Let's take search. If we know the top 150 search queries a customer makes related to our brand or topic, we can analyze this body of content and see exactly which people and organizations are shaping the experience our customers or citizens receive via Google or Bing. If you do this, you build a new "search media relations model" that will greatly impact search engine optimization. Do it well and you will save money on search and become far more effective. But don't expect the search team to make this recommendation. As a leader, you will have to push to see what is possible for every model.

Bad Actors Are Innovators Too: Unfortunately, they are improving as fast as we are. They are building bot networks from scratch to utilize Twitter, fool search engines, and guide people toward illicit goods, services, and ideas. They can alter voice, video, images, and language. The good news is they are just copying us, so if we become fluent in digital media, we will understand how they behave as well. That insight into the bad actors will become increasingly critical to avoid disruptions in sales and protect the reputations of our organizations and even ourselves.

Understand How Our Brains Work: We need to know how human brains develop from birth to age 25. This helps us see how habits and memories form and why certain psychological models dictate the effectiveness of our communications. In some cases, technologies will accentuate the importance of one psychological model over another, but the models that truly drive us don't really change. We should be as fluent in these psychological models as we are in reading a financial statement.

Content

The Media Game Has Changed Forever: Television to social is already the new norm worldwide. The mobile phone is the center of the universe for the global audience and print's effectiveness is diminishing. The largest media platform on earth is Facebook, with 2. 2 billion users.

The largest learning center on earth is Google, on which 63,000 searches are performed per second. Modern media looks social, acts social, and demands we do it all on the small screens of our smartphones. Our future innovations will occur in social media platforms (how we narrate life) and in messaging platforms (how we reach people in private environments). We need to think deeply about how that impacts the ways we create content.

The Best Creative Is Insights-Driven: The best chief creative officers will rely on insights as their foundation, and then innovate from that platform. We might still get those brilliant ideas in the shower, but only after consuming primary research and online data that show how our customers think. We'll make Sam Walton proud.

A Content-Planning Revolution: We can now build profiles of audiences we want to reach, create normative data sets of more than one million people, and figure out which micro-segments matter to our brand or organization. If we market a movie, we might look at 5,000 micro-segments, rather than the traditional set of customer personas developed via primary research. This new style of analysis, which flips the traditional market-segmentation model on its head, shows us how like-minded people find each other and reveals their common interests beyond the brand (e.g., media outlets, people, and content). It comes down to basic common sense: We all hang out in small groups, so let's identify those groups online.

Delivery

The 1-9-90 Model: The world's most important media model shows how we work and live online. We can see how influencers, sharers, and search intersect and how earned, shared, owned, and paid media now work together in different and more powerful ways. Every consumer plays a role in shaping the story of a brand, topic, or organization. Some are content creators (1%), some share to inform their communities (9%), and the rest benefit from the 1% and the 9%, passively consuming content via search, social, or mainstream media channels (90%). The future precision to know exactly which role each person plays will change the game.

Evaluation

Look Outside Your Comfort Zone: By studying countries from Pakistan to Germany, we start to see trends developing outside the United States and how they might impact us in the future. Entrepreneurs in China are often more innovative than we give them credit for. The same thing happens across industries, as well. Look out for and analyze the trends outside your own industry, so you don't get locked into the navel-gazing common in most sectors. Staring at your competitors is a path to mediocrity. Look at other industries and other countries and even bad actors to see what is possible. Too often, we refer to perfectly curated case studies. Push yourself to identify trends more quickly by evaluating what's happening outside of your normal worldview.

When You Turn Around, Is Your Team Behind You? The internal world should be treated with the same discipline and respect as your customers. How do we apply external techniques to the internal world of an organization? What common types of communications within organizations have very little chance for success, and how can we change this paradigm to inspire, educate, and shape the behavior of our own employees? It's time for us to admit that cascading, surveys, and other similar tools don't work well. How we adopt technology internally so that the internal experience resembles the external moves us a long way toward success.

In the years ahead, we will have more opportunity than ever to make a difference in the lives of our citizens, build stronger relationships with our customers, and help to shape a society we can be proud of each and every day.

To get there, we are reminded yet again of the wisdom of Sam Walton, who thought about how to do the right thing for his customers 24/7. His worldview was filled with wisdom that was common sense—yet many find it hard to replicate. One thing he said has always resonated with us: "There is only one boss: the customer. And he can fire everybody in the company from the chairman on down, simply by spending his money somewhere else."

We, as leaders, need to stay focused on what we can achieve, how we can gain new insights, and how our most powerful stories can inspire every audience filled with our bosses. We consider you, our reader, to be our "boss," and we welcome your feedback. We invite you to send comments and examples of both good and bad communication to info@craftingpersuasion.com so we can include them in future editions of this book and on our website: www.craftingpersuasion.com.

As the Chinese philosopher Lao Tzu said more than 2,500 years ago, "The journey of a thousand miles begins with one step." We hope this book and our website will help serve you as a critical first step in crafting well-considered, persuasive communication strategies. As long as you remember to put strategy ahead of execution, you are already well ahead of whomever you compete against in winning the hearts and minds of your target audience.

We look forward to learning from you as we continue our shared journey toward better understanding and effective communication between all of us.

Acknowledgements

Ken Blanchard, the author of 60 books, including the *One Minute Manager*, once said "none of us is as smart as all of us."

We couldn't agree more.

This book is a reflection of the generous sharing of expertise by our fellow professors, who agreed to interrupt otherwise busy lives to teach as part of the U.S. Marketing Communication College (USMCC).

Starting in August 2008, we have been joined by Jim Nyce, Mike Ribero, Gary Briggs, Elana Gold, Rachel Makool, Griff Griffity, Nigel Hollis, Matt Ackley, Shawn Mielke, Mark Kleinman, Eureka Ranch, Norm Levy, Cassidy Dale, David Knight, Gordon Wyner, Klon Kitchen, Victoria Romero, Kelly Hlavinka, George Perlov, Mike Linton, Dave Wallinga, Stan Slap, Andrea Cherng, Rob Malcolm, Terry Villines, Nancy Zwiers, Tim Love, Pete Carter and Kimberly Doebereiner.

Of course, none of this happens without strong coordination on the State Department side, as well. We would like to thank the entire team who has been involved. Their counsel and support have always been appreciated.

When we decided to write this book with three authors, we realized that a great editing team was the other missing ingredient. We are grateful for the literary prowess of Dan Zehr and Sarah Courteau, who helped us weave together *Crafting Persuasion*. For Bob and Dan, this is their fourth book as a team.

Of course, a book is just a bunch of words until we design the cover, figure out the interior layout and much more. We are thankful for Tamara Dever and Monica Thomas of TLC Graphics, who continue as the "hidden secret" behind 1845 Publishing's third book.

Vanessa Hess played a pivotal role, as she always does, in ensuring we were on Amazon.com, that our Kindle and e-book were created, and she took great care of logistics that make it possible for our readers to receive our book. We also are thankful for Justin Cato, Matt McCullough and the Ripcord Digital team for creating our website.

Last, but not least, we are thankful to our families and, in particular, our wives, for their encouragement and their patience as we engaged in weekly conference calls to discuss the content and quite a few sessions to edit and proofread the final product. If Zoom has a frequent user program, we are surely near the top of the list.

We hope you enjoy our book and visit us at www.craftingpersuasion.com. Let us know what you think and share ideas with us for the future.

Sincerely,
Kip, Ed and Bob

About the Authors

Kip Knight is an Operating Partner at Thomvest Ventures based in San Francisco and is also Founder of CMO Coaches. This is his first book. Kip has served in a variety of marketing and senior management roles at Procter & Gamble, PepsiCo, YUM Brands, eBay, and H&R Block. His work has enabled him to work in over 60 countries around the world. He currently serves on two boards (Netbase and 5-11 Tactical). Kip splits his time between Orange County and the Bay area in California with his wife, Peggy. They have two sons, Tom and Chris.

Ed Tazzia is a principal at Sycamore and Company a management consulting firm which specializes in executive search, innovation mentoring and executive training. He started his career at Procter & Gamble and serves as global Chairman of the 36,000-member P&G Alumni Network. His experience ranges from the North American Soccer league, to Campbell's Soup's Vlasic Division, to IBM. His first book was Starting Over, a guide to a job search. Ed lives in Michigan with his wife Julie and they have two daughters, Gennie and Samantha.

Bob Pearson has helped build two major consulting firms, GCI Health and W2O Group, and has served as head of global communications for Novartis, Dell and Sanofi (Rhone-Poulenc Rorer). He created the Fortune 500's first global social media function at Dell. An author of four books, Bob is adjunct professor at The University of Texas at Austin McCombs School for Business, Syracuse University and is a Visiting Scholar at The University of Southern California. Bob resides in Austin, Texas with his wife, Donna.